Praise for
Jerry Weintraub and

WHEN I STOP TALKING
YOU'LL KNOW I'M DEAD

"Fascinating...[Weintraub] is breezily forthcoming about his life as a legendary concert promoter, movie producer, Broadway show producer, actor, philanthropist, best pal to George Clooney and president George H.W. Bush, author, and most of all, survivor."
—*Chicago Sun-Times*

"Drops more boldface names than a gossip column...As the title of the book indicates, Weintraub loves to talk. And the seventy-two-year-old impresario has some amazing stories to tell...all told in Weintraub's shooting-the-breeze voice."
—Rick Warner, *Bloomberg News*

"Edgy and honest but refreshingly spare in his criticism of stars, colleagues, and family...With a bold voice, a storied career, and a cast of superstars, Weintraub's memoir makes a rousing insider tour of some five decades in the entertainment industry."
—*Publishers Weekly*

"Full of great stories." —*Wall Street Journal*

"The classic self-made Hollywood tale, as it's been molded by Warners, Zanucks, and Geffens...Old chestnuts from this journey are lovingly, and often hilariously, burnished...The book, which is in no way a scandalous showbiz tell-all but a good-humored, and often self-deprecating, romp of outrageous will and amazing fortune, also paints a picture of uncanny bliss."
—Nicole LaPorte, *The Daily Beast*

"FOUR STARS…This is a guy who can tell a story. And boy does he have stories to tell. The legendary producer was around for—or created—cultural moments with Elvis and Sinatra, not to mention Brad P. and George C. A nice Jewish boy from the Bronx, Weintraub became a political force and pal of presidents; the elder Bush, then a senator, got him into a restricted country club. Weintraub exhibits no false modesty—or illusions."

—*People*

"Page-turning…now it's Hollywood producer Jerry Weintraub's turn to take center stage and shine like a star…As much as telling the story of his life, the memoir offers wisdom for others hoping to follow his path." —Reuters

"Now, I could tell you stories about Jerry, but Jerry is the first and best to tell them. He's funny and grumpy and perfectly inappropriate. When it comes to work, nobody works harder. When it comes to charities, nobody guilts better. And when it comes to friendship, he has no peers. That's Jerry's great talent. He doesn't just light up a room, he lights it on fire. He's a great producer, a great organizer, a great friend, and truly the greatest showman on earth." —George Clooney

"For more than five decades [Weintraub] has been a larger-than-life manager, promoter, producer, and legendary impresario for a *Forbes* list of the great and powerful…aside from the fact that he's a notoriously great storyteller and there are loads of intimate stories about the biggest names in show business, there is an emotional narrative that drives the story—a chance to see what it's like behind the curtain with the wizard."

—*Sunday Times Magazine* (London)

"Required reading." —*New York Post*

"Jerry has made a fascinating career for himself…bloomed wherever he's been planted. His life has put him in the company of greats like Elvis Presley, Frank Sinatra, The Rat Pack, Robert Altman, and Steven Soderbergh, to name a few. Jerry's story chronicles his journey that involved a lot of improvising, love, and, of course, luck. This story isn't just for music or movie lovers, or entrepreneurs…it's for everyone…If there was a Mount Rushmore of legendary show business figures, he'd be one of them."

—Don Imus

"A lively and endearing memoir by one of the last men standing from a certain golden age of the entertainment industry."

—*Heritage Florida Jewish News*

"Weintraub worked with Elvis and Sinatra. He headed a studio. And now he's written a memoir that's also a how-to guide…WHEN I STOP TALKING, YOU'LL KNOW I'M DEAD is anything but a rote, let-the-record-show memoir…it's written with stealth and style, doubtless shaped by his co-writer, Rich Cohen…The book really is a performance, a monologue by a guy comfortable hanging with Armand Hammer at Leonid Brezhnev's funeral or with Joey Bishop at a deli."

—RJ Smith, *Los Angeles Times*

"Between Mr. Weintraub's skills as a raconteur, Rich Cohen's punchy style as his co-writer, and a fabulous cast of those with whom Mr. Weintraub has done business over the years, this book is paved wall to wall with funny, hard-nosed stories…he's great at the name-dropping game: 'Yeah, *Elvis*. It's me. What's up?' Even in that kind of company his best stories are the ones about himself."

—Janet Maslin, *New York Times*

"In the book's most entertaining stories he not only has to sell an audience on a celebrity but also has to sell the celebrity on himself... 'I'll tell you my biggest talent,' says Weintraub. 'When I believe in something, it's going to get done.' No reader of his memoir will need to be convinced of that."

—Nathaniel Rich, *Vanity Fair*

"Truth is often more outrageous than fiction, especially when you consider Jerry Weintraub's outrageous fortune. As a young man, he booked nationwide tours for Elvis Presley and Frank Sinatra. In the process, he reinvented their careers and changed the business of live music."   —National Public Radio

"He sold Elvis to the masses, staged Sinatra's comeback. And has the biggest stars on his speed dial. When celebrities want something done, he's the man. Hollywood producer, power player. And author of a terrific memoir... What a man, what a book."   —Larry King

WHEN I STOP TALKING, YOU'LL KNOW I'M DEAD

Useful Stories from a Persuasive Man

JERRY WEINTRAUB

WITH RICH COHEN

TWELVE

New York   Boston

To Rose and Sam Weintraub,
without whom none of this
would have been possible, and
of course, Jane and Susie.

Twelve
Hachette Book Group
237 Park Avenue
New York, NY 10017

www.HachetteBookGroup.com

Twelve is an imprint of Grand Central Publishing.
The Twelve name and logo are trademarks of Hachette Book Group, Inc.

The publisher is not responsible for websites (or their content) that are not owned by the publisher.

Printed in the United States of America

Originally published in hardcover by Twelve

First Trade Edition: March 2011
10 9 8 7 6 5 4 3 2

The Library of Congress has cataloged the hardcover edition as follows:

Weintraub, Jerry.
    When I stop talking, you'll know I'm dead : useful stories from a persuasive man / Jerry Weintraub with Rich Cohen. —1st ed.
        p. cm.
    Includes index.
    ISBN 978-0-446-54815-1
  1. Weintraub, Jerry.   2. Motion picture producers and directors—United States—Biography.   I. Cohen, Rich.   II. Title.
    PN1998.3.W435 A3 2010
    791.4302'32092—dc22
    [B]
                                                            2009049494

ISBN 978-0-446-54816-8 (pbk.)

12/24/76

There once was a kid with a dream
Whose vision was clear and supreme
He formed Management Three
And quick as can be
The dream became one with his scheme

First there was Denver and eventually Frank
Followed by Dorothy & Neil
His Rep. it did grow
And as we all know
Others came wanting to deal

He was man of the year,
"The Wiz of the Biz,"
And accolades too many to count
The dream and the scheme
Turned to bread and to cream
Success it continued to mount

The end of this rhyme is near.
Weintraub is really a dear.
When he's needed most
No more gracious a host,
No more generous a man is there—

With much love and appreciation,

Bob Dylan

CONTENTS

Contents

Introduction

This book is not the story of my entire life, nor is it the catalogue of my every adventure. It is not meant to exhaust every era nor chronicle every detail. It is instead a tour of just those select moments of hilarity or epiphany—at home and in the office, in the bedroom, studio, and arena—that pushed me this way or that and gave my life direction. The crucial hours, that's what I am after. I also mean it as a chronicle and tribute to some of the great figures of my time, the few I influenced and the many who influenced me. I have been fortunate to have known more than a couple of great people and to have worked with more than a couple of great artists. The story of these people, men and women, is the story of my age, and I consider myself fortunate to have been born in the right nation with the right parents at the right moment. In short, this book, if it is working, should read less like a text than like a conversation, a late-night talk in which a man who likes to talk and happens to have been alive a long time and had his nose in everything tells you of the high points, the grand moments, and the stunning incidents when everything was sharp and clear. I sometimes think a person is a kind of memory machine. You collect, and sort, and remember, then you tell. Looking back—and telling is nothing but look-ing back—I have come away with a profound sense of humil-ity. I suppose this comes from recognizing my life as a pattern, a cohesive collection of incidents whose author I cannot quite discern. In other words, the more I live, the more amazed I am by living. And maybe that's right. As G–D says in an old book, "What you have been given is yours to understand, but the rest belongs to me."

The Star of Ardaban

I have a philosophy of life, but I don't live by it and never could practice it. Now, at seventy-two, I realize every minute doing one thing is a minute not doing something else, every choice is another choice not made, another path grown over and lost. If asked my philosophy, it would be simply this: Savor life, don't press too hard, don't worry too much. Or as the old-timers say, "Enjoy." But, as I said, I never could live by this philosophy and was, in fact, out working, hustling, trading, scheming, and making a buck as soon as I was old enough to leave my parents' house.

When I was ten, Robert Mitchum was arrested in the cold-water flat across the street from our apartment in the Bronx. I remember Robert Mitchum as the husky, sleepy-eyed actor who played all those noirish roles that told you there was something not so squeaky clean in Bing Crosby's America, but Mitchum got those parts only after the arrest, in which he was caught in bed with two girls in the middle of the day smoking dope. No small scandal. In those days, merely staying in bed till 9:00 A.M. was considered suspicious. It would have been the end of his career if not for some genius movie producer who realized all that public disgust could be harnessed by repackaging the actor into a dark, interesting, complicated character.

When the story broke, the parents in my neighborhood went wild. *The schanda! This matinee idol picks our block to engage in his immorality?* The yentas went up and down the street, wailing. One of the mothers on Jerome Avenue grabbed me by the collar and said, "Jerry, you're the younger generation, an American boy, what do you think of this actor with his chippies and his Mexican cigarette?"

I smiled with my hand out, because I had just made a delivery and was waiting for a tip. "I'll never see another one of his movies," I told her. "He has shamed not just our neighborhood, but all of the Bronx."

Then, to tease her, I said, "And did you hear? He's Jewish!"

"No! It can't be, you're joking."

"No joke. My brother Melvyn says they pulled tefillin and a prayer book out of that dirty little room."

"Oh, God, I'm going to faint!"

"Not yet," I said, waving my hand. And the purse came out, followed by a few well-circulated nickels.

Of course, I wasn't really disgusted by Robert Mitchum's behavior. I was awed. What did I think? I applauded the man. In bed with two women in the middle of the day? That's the dream! That's Hollywood!

I was born in Brooklyn, raised in the Bronx. When people ask where I'm from, I always say Brooklyn, though I spent only my earliest years in the borough. Brooklyn because when you hear the Bronx you think baseball, vacant lots, tenement fires, whereas, when you hear Brooklyn, you think guys. In my oldest memories, I am on the street, with a roving pack of kids. We hung out beneath the Jerome Avenue El, where the shadows made complicated patterns. The sidewalks were lined with Irish and Italian bars. On my way to school, I would see the drunks at their stools, having their first shots of the day. We stayed out there for hours, talking about what we wanted. We played stickball and stoopball, the Spalding bounding off the third step of the brownstone, arcing against the beams of the elevated. When a train went by, it rained sparks. If you listened to us, you would not have understood half of it, everything being in nicknames, slang, and code. My brother Melvyn was (and is) my best friend, two years younger, not a resentful bone in his body, though he had to pay for my sins in school: *Mel Weintraub? Jerry's brother? You sit in back and keep your mouth shut.*

The neighborhood was bounded by big roads to the south and the Hudson River to the west, with a distant view of the Palisades. Manhattan was just a twenty-minute subway ride, but a light-year, away. At night, when the IRT train went over Jerome Avenue, its windows aglow, I dreamed of going to the city. I was impatient to see the world. Now and then, tired of gray days in the classroom, I cut school and instead caught a train to Times Square, where I sat through two features and a floor show at the Roxy or the Paramount or one of the other grand show palaces. The velvet curtains, the plush aisles, the stars and stage sets and glamour—this is where I fell in love with movies. *Back to Bataan* with Robert Taylor; *Pursued* with Robert Mitchum; *Here Comes Mr. Jordan* with Robert Montgomery; *Fort Apache* with John Wayne; *The Beautiful Blonde from Bashful Bend* with Betty Grable, with that body and those legs, each insured for a million dollars by Lloyd's of London. This was not a theater; it was a synagogue. Everything I wanted was up on the screen.

There is nothing better than coming out of a movie on a summer night when the sun is still in the sky. I would take the train back to 174th Street and wander through the neighborhood, past the Chinese laundry, druggist, newsstand, smoke shop, deli, with scenes from the movie flickering in my mind— gun battles, chases, immortal bits of dialogue. *I'll get you, you dirty rat.* I would toss off my coat as I came in the door, overwhelmed by the smells from the kitchen, where my mother was cooking one of her great Eastern European dishes. It gave me so much, just knowing she was back there, at home, worrying and waiting; a sense of security; a sense that the world has order, and will continue tomorrow as it is today.

When I was very young, we lived in an apartment house at 47 Featherbed Lane. Later, when my father made some money, we moved to a place on the Grand Concourse. Once a month, the landlord drove up in his Cadillac to collect the rent. There were very few cars on the streets in those days, the causeways and lanes being left to hooligans and mothers and rollicking kids. Which made the arrival of the landlord, this scary man in the long black car, as dramatic as a scene in a movie. I mean, there we were, out playing ball, when all of a sudden, here it comes, shiny and metallic black, a block long, with the landlord inside. He was a German and spoke with an accent. We could see him through the glass, with his account books and change purse, puffed up with this huge, godly ability to collect and reject and toss you out of your house. He may have been the nicest man in the world, but we feared him. At the first glint of his grille, we ran into our homes and hid under our beds.

We lived on the second floor because my mother was afraid of heights. I spent hours on the fire escape watching the traffic, the people in the street. I had relatives all over the neighborhood. I used to lie awake after bedtime, listening to my uncles tell stories about the legendary gonifs and bootleggers who ran the Bronx long ago. I had one grandfather who was a communist. He used to stand on a soap box in Union Square decrying the fat cats and was arrested once a week. I had another grandfather who was a union organizer. He wore a suit and a tie and smoked a cigar. All my relatives talked all the time but it was always the same story: the old country, the crossing, the struggle, the dream.

My mother's name was Rose. She had reddish-brown hair and looked Irish. (I used to tell people my real name was O'Hara, that Weintraub had been invented for business purposes.) She grew up in Brooklyn, where she had been as cloistered as any of the nuns at St. Mary's. I don't think she had been anywhere or done anything before she met my father. Like a lot of the Jewish women of that era, she went straight from the house of her parents to the house of her husband. The first time she ate a lobster—I remember my father bringing the forbidden sea monsters into the house—she tried to crack the shell and sent a claw sailing across the room. What did she care about delicacies? Protecting us, keeping us from the suffering of the world, that was her task. She did not want us to know about the existence of hospitals, let alone mortuaries. If I had a relative who suddenly stopped coming to the apartment and I asked, "Where is Uncle Dave?" She would say, "Dave went on a trip." Then, three years would go by and I would ask, "What happened to Uncle Dave?" And she'd say, "Oh, Uncle Dave died years ago."

She was a beautiful woman, with all the magical powers we boys attribute to our mothers: She was always there, watching and praising, supporting, loving, beaming. She was parochial, scared of a lot of things, but fought through her fear for our sake. She was afraid of heights, as I said. She was also afraid of cars, airplanes, restaurants, basically the whole world beyond New York City. Her struggle—the battle between her fear and her desire to raise sons who were without fear—was dramatized on a trip we took out West, when my father decided we should take the tourist train to the top of Pike's Peak in Colorado. We got our tickets, took our seats, and around and around we went, up Jacob's Ladder to heaven. My mother was smiling and nodding the entire way, but her knuckles were white and tears streamed down her face. It said something about human will, or about a mother's love, or maybe it was really about the stubbornness of my father, who said, "We're doing this, and that is all there is to it."

His name was Samuel, and he was the perfect match for my mother. Where she was parochial and nervous (most comfortable inside the apartment), he was worldly and sophisticated (most comfortable out in the world). He was a salesman, and had been on the road since he was fourteen. She worked as a secretary in his office. He had crossed the country a half dozen times before they met, had friends in dozens of states, was welcomed everywhere he went. He used to return from trips with stories and souvenirs. Postcards, trinkets, tchotchkes—the romance of these things lingered in the apartment. If I caused him trouble later on, if I banged into him while trying to get free—and believe me, I was a big, mischievous pain in the ass—my father can blame himself. He was the one who filled me with dreams of the greater world. I simply wanted to see what he had seen.

My father was in the jewelry business. He bought and sold gems. Following years of struggle, he started to do okay after World War II, when refugees began to arrive from Europe, many with a stash of jewels they needed to sell. My father began as a kind of middleman, but ultimately built a thriving business.

I remember him leaving for India, Paris, Ceylon. He would hunt the markets and bazaars for rubies, sapphires, diamonds. He had a beautiful suitcase and was a fantastic packer, shirts and pants folded into special compartments, pockets for papers, pockets for notebooks and cigars. He would hug Melvyn before he left, then say, "Take care of them, Jerry. You're the man of the house now."

When I was eight years old, my father returned from a trip with the largest star sapphire in the world. It was a piece of junk, picked up from a secondhand dealer. He polished it, then did something that made an impression on me. He named it. He called it "The Star of Ardaban." Why give a name to this old piece of nothing? Because it's not the gem a person buys. It's the story behind the gem. It's the romance. He had a special case made for the Star of Ardaban, the sort of case you might carry handcuffed to your wrist. He took a trip, traveling with the Star of Ardaban across the country. In each town, he was met at the train station by armed guards, a Brinks truck, and a local reporter. A few days later, after the story appeared in the local paper, he would invite all the jewelers to his hotel room to look at the Star of Ardaban. Then, as they were examining the Star of Ardaban, he was selling them everything else in his jewelry case. At the end of the tour, he donated the Star to the Smithsonian. It's there to this day.

This is a Bible story in my family, a foundational myth—it explains everything you need to know about my father's business and about my own. Though he was selling rubies and sapphires and I am selling Clooney, Pitt, and Damon, the trick is the same: packaging. You might have the greatest talent in the world, but it doesn't matter if you can't sell it. Am I Richard Rodgers, Stephen Sondheim, Saul Bellow, Ernest Hemingway? No. I can't write a novel. I can't write a play. I can't write a song. But I can help the artist get that book or song or play noticed by the public. And that's packaging. When you dig through all the craziness of my life, you'll see that I'm just a guy from the Bronx who knows how to attract a crowd. I can get people to notice the sapphire, so it's not lying in a cellar where it might be found in a hundred years, long after the man who mined it has died. That is my talent. If I had been around with Van Gogh or Melville, they would not have had to wait so long for fame.

When I was nine, my father took us to California. He wanted to show me and my brother the world outside the Bronx, and he wanted my mother to see Hollywood. She was crazy for the movies, one of those ladies you would see in an empty theater on the Grand Concourse, a box of tissues on her lap, weeping. (She named my brother not after some long-lost shtetl-dwelling ancestor but for one of her favorite actors, Melvyn Douglas, a star of *Captains Courageous*.) We loaded up the car and crossed the George Washington Bridge into America. Route 22 to 15, Pennsylvania, Ohio, Illinois. I pressed my face to the window, watching the towns go by. We slept in motels, ate in diners, visited tourist traps. I saw cowboys, horses, and distant peaks white in the smoky freight-yard dawn. I was a baby but already felt the pull of forces greater than myself, older even than my grandparents, a feeling that is with me even when I am alone. We stopped in Las Vegas. This was soon after the war. The town was nothing, a desert nowhere in which midcentury hoodlums were sketching plans for palaces. I would later spend much of my life there, with Elvis, Sinatra, the Colonel, put on so many shows and ink so many deals, and here I was, years earlier, ghosting through this nothing place. I was a child and Vegas was a child, but we would grow up, and meet again.

We arrived in LA at dawn. My father was driving, window open, sleeves rolled back. "Jerry, wake up—you're gonna want to see this." I opened my eyes as we came over the hill. I could see the buildings of downtown, the hills behind them, the ocean behind that. The light was so pure it was white, catching the tops of the towers, which glowed in the sun. It would be great if you could preserve the first vision of a place that would become important to you, but later experience gets tangled up with memory until what came later changes what came before. You can never really save anything. We stayed in the Roosevelt Hotel on Hollywood Boulevard, across from Grauman's Chinese Theater, where the stars have their hand and footprints in cement. I spent an afternoon there, measuring myself against Humphrey Bogart, Jimmy Stewart, Gregory Peck, all of whom, for whatever reason, had surprisingly small feet.

About three years ago, after *Ocean's Thirteen* premiered, the people who run Grauman's said they wanted the stars of the film—Brad Pitt, Matt Damon, George Clooney—to put their prints in the cement. Clooney said, "Look, we'll do it, but Jerry has to do it, too." As a rule, Grauman's only honors actors, but they really wanted these guys, so they relented. As I was putting my hands in the cement, I looked up and saw the very window in the Roosevelt Hotel from which, all those years ago, I had looked out at Hollywood. While I was thinking about this—how strange to return to the same place, only now on the other side of the glass—I noticed the men next to me, my friends, were laughing.

A few days earlier, Clooney had called Pitt and Damon and said, "You know how when you go to Grauman's the footprints always look so small? Well, you don't want a kid out there, years from now, saying, 'Oh, God, look at Brad Pitt and Matt Damon—they had baby feet!' Tell you what. I'll pick us up size fourteen shoes, three pairs. Jerry? Oh, well, let's not mention it to Jerry." So these friends of mine have clown shoes, while I'm the guy with the tiny feet on the walk of fame. And you know what they say about small feet.

My father drove us all over LA. One night, we waited in front of a spot on Sunset Boulevard where the stars showed themselves. I think it was Ciro's. You have to understand what it was like back then. There were few cars on Sunset, no high-rises. It was still woods and wilderness, cactus fronds from the last joint all the way to the ocean. Beverly Hills was a country town. The clubs on Sunset sat in the middle of all that wilderness like a string of pearls. This was before TV, before anything. It was olden times, when the studio bosses, in need of publicity, would scheme their way into the news, which usually meant dressing their stars in finery and sending them, in matching couples, before the flashbulbs along the red carpets of Sunset.

So we stood in front of Ciro's, with the sun going down. The cars rolled up and the stars walked the carpet, frozen in the light of the flash, *pop, pop, pop.* The door opened and I caught a glimpse of smoke and swells and bubbles, a look inside the genie bottle. (I thought I had died and gone to heaven.) Standing out there, on the wrong side of the rope, seeing the stars disappear into the velvet interior—well, if that doesn't make you ambitious, nothing will.

I remember Joan Crawford coming out with her head down, throwing her arms up, turning it on, slipping into her car, a boat of a thing. There was a boyfriend, but she was driving. I remember Mickey Cohen, too, the gangster who ran the underworld. He was a pug of a guy, rough looking but shedding more wattage than any of the film stars. Mickey was shot soon after. (He recovered.) My father showed me the story in the paper. As I read the story, I imagined the strutting strongman, grinning in the paparazzi flash. That was Hollywood to me—starlets and gangsters, glamour and menace and a snubnose .38 going *blam blam blam*.

There was a guy named Delmer Daves, a fascinating guy, a movie guy, a writer and director and producer, who started in the business as a prop boy on a silent called *Covered Wagon*. I won't go into tremendous detail about Delmer Daves, except to say he was a Stanford-educated lawyer, lived with the Hopi Indians, made a half dozen classic films, and was interested in jewelry, which is how he came to know my father. When he heard we were in LA, he invited us to lunch at the Fox studio. I remember the day vividly. Driving to the gate, the guard checking the list for "Weintraub," the thrill of being on that list, our name among the names of actors and movie people. The lot was a hubbub of activity—these were the days of the old studio system, when everything important happened on those few acres. It was a circus, with extras in cowboy hats and chaps and conquistador helmets and spurs, starlets in gowns, cameras and microphones and the machinery of show business. And the sets, little glimpses of Paris and New York, alleys and stoops rebuilt to the smallest detail—the street lamp, the park bench, the window from which your mother calls—so perfect beneath the clean, Pacific sky.

We ate in the commissary. Daves talked with my father. Everywhere I looked, I saw stars. At one table, Betty Grable was in costume, killing time as the cameras were moved for the next shot. She wore a sheer dress, and, of course, my eyes went straight to those beautiful legs. She was eating a sandwich, drinking a soda. I could not take my eyes off her. As she was eating and drinking, and as I was watching, she belched. It might sound like nothing, but to me it came as an epiphany. Those beautiful legs. *And she belched!* It upset me, and elated me, too. It meant these big stars were just people, normal human beings. It meant I could live here someday, be one of them. I told Betty Grable about this years later, that my career was made possible by her belch—I don't think it thrilled her. She smiled and said, "Well, Jerry, I'm glad I could help."

My father took us to Beverly Hills so we could see where the movie stars lived. It was nothing then, just a sleepy little town, as I said, filled with mom-and-pop stores. We went through the roads above Sunset Boulevard, where mansions clung to the cliffs. In my memory, every house is midcentury Spanish with porticos and overlooks and guest cabanas and side porches where the desert wind blows through the Joshua trees and cypress. I live in one of these houses now. I've had it remodeled, but you can still see the bones of old Beverly Hills. (Imagine a madcap silent screen star wandering in the halls, getting drunk on champagne, wrecking her coupe then calling the studio head to keep it out of the papers.) I bought it in the early 1970s, in a moment of success. It is just the sort of place I imagined an old-time studio great might live, Harry Cohn, David O. Selznick, or Irving Thalberg. It's where I'm writing these pages, telling these stories, each on its own an anecdote, but together the life of the kid with a dream looking back when the dream has come true.

I graduated from P.S. 70 a few weeks before the trip, and had brought along my autograph book, which is what we had instead of a yearbook. I waved it at every celebrity I met—on the carpet at Ciro's, on the Fox Lot, in Beverly Hills. I carried it to the doors of several mansions. Just walked right up and rang the bell. (If you tried this today, you'd be "neutralized," a burlap sack would be thrown over your head and you'd be hurried off to a secret location.) I still have that old autograph book. It's like something from another age, small, green, filled with signatures—some from teachers, some from classmates, some from movie stars. Carmen Miranda, Bette Davis, Paul Douglas, each of whom added a few words of encouragement. "Keep going, Jerry!" "You'll make it, Jerry!" "You'll be great, Jerry!" Years later, when I met some of these people again, I showed them the book. And they laughed. Betty Grable wanted to take a pen and add, "You're welcome for the belch, Jerry." I told her not to do it. You really shouldn't tamper with a historical document.

The Red Jacket

I did not like school. I was crazy about sports, especially football, and liked girls, and being around other kids, but the classrooms, where you had to sit and listen because the teachers were in charge—not for me. Maybe I thought I knew too much, had too clear a picture of the world and its hierarchies and where public school teachers fit into those hierarchies. I sat by the windows in back of class, looking over the rooftops of the Bronx, the chimneys and pipes. Beyond school was the Grand Concourse, beyond the Grand Concourse was Manhattan. I was impatient to see the world, and thus a usual suspect for the truant officer. I would look into the hall before first period, sign the sign-in sheet, then take off. Hurrying across the avenue with my collar pulled high to cover my face, I would run up the steps to the platform of the elevated. The D train was my limousine as it tottered and wheezed its way into the city.

One afternoon, I saw a red jacket in a store window on Mt. Eden Avenue, just around the corner from our apartment. That red jacket changed everything. It was worn by a mannequin, in a casual, hanging-out, street-corner pose. It was an exact replica of the one James Dean wore in *Rebel Without a Cause*. I imagined myself slouching in it, leaning in doorways in it, speaking bits of tough, cynical dialogue in it. (*All the time! I don't know what gets into me—but I keep looking for trouble and I always—I swear you better lock me up. I'm going to smash somebody—I know it.*) I took it off the mannequin and slipped it over my shoulders. It fit like a glove and hummed like a wire. It was the most beautiful thing I had ever seen. I had to have it. This was the first time I felt that consumerist urge: need it, need it, need it. I dug in my pockets. Nothing. Nada. Zilch. Sadness followed by determination. I went around the corner, got my father, and dragged him back to the store. He watched me take down the jacket, zip it up, and turn around, all the time nodding in approval. "Oh, yes, Jerry, that is a gorgeous coat. It looks great on you, too, like it was made for you."

"Can I get it?" I asked.

"Sure," he said, "do you have the money?"

"No," I told him. "Can't you buy it for me?"

"Oh, no, that's not how it works," he said. "You get a job, save your money, then *you* buy it. Then you'll enjoy it. Otherwise, it won't mean anything. You'll get tired of it in an hour."

It was the beginning of my life as a working man. I got the jacket, of course, wore it till I lost it, but, by then, the jobs I had taken to buy the jacket had become more important to me than the jacket itself had ever been. At some point, you forget the object, and the means becomes the end. You work for the joy of the work. My father must have known this would happen.

One of my first jobs was in a movie theater on 170th Street in the Bronx. I was fourteen years old. I had been sneaking into the place since I was a kid. You could swing onto the balcony from a fire escape. It was dangerous and exciting. One night, the manager caught me. His name was Mr. Allen, and he was a good guy. He could have called my parents, or the police, but instead said, "I know you sneak in here every day and see the same movies over and over. Why don't you just work as an usher?"

When I was thirteen, I got a job at Goldberg's, a resort in the Catskills. I started as a busboy but was soon promoted to waiter. One day, I was serving a big wheel named Abraham Levitt. This is the guy who built Levittown on Long Island. He invented the modern suburbs. He took an interest in me. He asked about my parents, my plans, my dreams. This has been a theme in my life: Somehow, I have attracted mentors. Again and again, who knows why, older men have taken me under their wing. Maybe they recognized something in me, a vision of their younger selves, before their wife left them, before they were disappointed by their children, whatever. "Why are you working here?" Mr. Levitt asked. "Why aren't you at the Concord or Grossinger's? The big places. You're never going to make any money at Goldberg's."

I told him I did not know anybody at the Concord or Grossinger's.

"Don't worry," he said. "I'll take care of you."

The next morning, he drove me over to the Concord and introduced me to the owner, Arthur Winarick, and to his children. They gave me a job at the pool. At night, I danced with the girls. I went there for years, first as a cabana boy, then as a guest, finally as a talent agent. Relationships are the only thing that really matters, in business and in life. That's what I learned from Abraham Levitt.

I started my first business around this time. It began with a sudden realization, an insight. There was a dry cleaner's on the ground floor of our apartment building. It was owned by a man named Angelo Bozanellis. I used to sit on the fire escape of our apartment and watch the men get off the train and rush into the store, then head home with their dry cleaning. I went to Mr. Bozanellis and said, "I can't stand to watch these men struggle every night. Do us all a favor. Let me deliver the cleaning. That way, a man comes home from work, he goes directly to see his wife and children. Maybe we'll save a marriage."

He said yes.

I asked what I would get paid.

"You'll make money on tips. People will give you nickels and dimes. But you gotta hustle. It's up to you."

Fine.

I made my deliveries every day at four, racing though the neighborhood, up and down stairs, in and out of the little, tomblike elevators, delivering the dry cleaning to housewives an hour before their husbands came home. One afternoon, I saw a regular customer coming out of the Chinese laundry with a sack of clothes, and then it hit me. The same people who were having their cleaning done were also having their clothes washed. So I went in and spoke to the owner, Louie Hong, an old Chinese man with dark, mysterious eyes. I said, "Look, Mr. Hong, as long as I'm delivering the cleaning, I might as well bring the wash, too. It's going to the same houses."

Just like that, I had become an entrepreneur.

But I had done a stupid thing. It did not take me long to realize my mistake. No matter how many packages I carried up the stairs, the tip stayed the same. There must be a business-school term for this: I was competing against myself, driving down my own prices. I figured out a solution. I would carry everything up in one trip, but hide the washing under the landing. First I would deliver just the dry cleaning, then loop back later to deliver the laundry. This way, I got two dimes instead of one.

Over time, the neighborhood took on a different aspect for me. I saw it with new eyes. It was no longer just streets and stores: It was needs and opportunities, money to be made. Once you see the world this way, things are never the same. It is like recognizing the pattern in the carpet. You cannot unrecognize it. The grocery, the fruit stand, the newspaper seller—I was making deliveries for all of them. Very quickly, there was too much business to handle on my own. I went to my brother and said, "Melvyn, I have a good thing going, but I need help." We recruited a half dozen kids from the corner, and I soon had a little army of delivery boys running all over the neighborhood, with a percentage of each tip sent up the chain to me.

I learned lessons from this business that I still follow today: People will pay you to make their lives easier; always take the time to make the pitch; personal service is the name of the game; never get paid once for doing something twice.

When I was fourteen years old, I ran away from home. I don't mean down the block away, or in the city overnight away, I mean *away*, away. I was standing on the corner with my friend Stuie Platt when the restlessness took hold of me.

"What do you say we get out of here?" I said.

"Out of here where?" he asked.

"Out of here, out of here," I said.

My uncle owned part of a hotel in Miami Beach. If we could make it down there, I figured he would give us bellhop jobs. In Miami Beach, being a bellhop is like being an aristocrat—that's what I told Stuie. We would earn pockets of cash parking Cadillac cars.

"How are we going to get there?" asked Stuie.

"We'll hitchhike," I said.

"How do you hitchhike to Florida?" he asked.

"What do you mean," I said, "You stick out your thumb—that's how."

We left with four dollars. We were on the road all day, eating in diners, resting on the median, the traffic breaking around us like surf. We had spent all the money by the time we reached Pennsylvania.

"How far to Florida?" asked Stuie.

"A few more days," I told him.

We got scared when the sun went down. We slept hugging each other in a field, but continued at dawn. Virginia, North Carolina, South Carolina. We were starving and broke. You know who fed us? Black people. In those days, the blacks were on one side of the street, the whites were on the other. On the white side, we were shooed away like rats, chased, cursed. On the black side, we were talked to, looked after, given plates piled with food. We would fill up and go on, skirting the wood shacks with dogs barking and the sun beating down.

Two drunk men in a red Oldsmobile convertible stopped for us outside Myrtle Beach, South Carolina. We climbed in back. Here is what I remember: one of the men asking me questions; the squeal of rubber; the things along the road—trees, houses, signs—spinning past us; the car sailing off the pavement; breaking glass; being thrown; being in the air; landing in a bed of soft, black dirt, dazed; something screaming toward me through the sky—HUMPH! It lands at my side. It's Stuie. We stare at each other, confused. We get up and run. Away from the road, the car and broken glass and the drunk men.

We went through the woods into Myrtle Beach. We were crying, heaving, little-kid sobs, all the way. We asked for the police station. A young cop with white teeth called our parents in the Bronx, then drove us to an airport on the edge of town. There was a big, silver plane on the runway—Capital Airlines. The propellers started with a cough and spun into a void. I sat at the window. We sped down the runway, lifted off—the town and the sea were soon far below us. It was the first time I had been on a plane.

We landed at LaGuardia. There was no terminal then. You parked in a field and walked. My mother and father were waiting. I could see my father's face. He was angry, pounding his fist into his palm, muttering, "Wait till I get my hands on him." My mother pushed down his fist, saying, "Don't you touch him. Don't you touch my boy."

Four days—that's how long we were gone, but those four days changed my life. Because I was scared but kept on going and managed to survive.

When we got home, my father sat me down and asked, "Why did you do it, Jerry?"

"Why? Because I wanted to see the world."

Everything but the Girl

I had no desire to go to college. I figured the world would be my classroom. Freshman year was the U.S. Air Force. I enlisted in the spring before high-school graduation. At seventeen, I was not old enough to sign the form, so I had to ask my parents for permission. My mother was distressed, but my father knew there was no holding me. "Sign it," he told her. "Just sign it."

Why the Air Force?

Because I did not think I could survive the Marine training, because I did not want to be an Army grunt, because I hated the Navy uniforms.

My basic training started at Sampson Air Force Base, in upstate New York, then continued at Kessler Air Force Base in Biloxi, Mississippi, where signs on the lawns near town said: "No niggers, no kikes, no dogs." What you learn in such a place is not just what they are teaching. I mean, yes, they taught me to work a radio, talk in code, sit in a bunker with earphones on my head, tracking jets across the sky, but what I learned was America, the South, people from other parts of the country, how to stand up and take care of myself.

I had a good old boy, son of a bitch sergeant named Harley. He used to mangle my name at mail call, really Jew it up: *WHINE*-traub! *WHINE*-traub! *WHINE*-traub! I got lots of letters from my high-school sweetheart—she became my first wife. She used to send cookies and candy. Harley would rip open the packages and throw the cookies all over the floor, yelling, *WHINE*-traub! *WHINE*-traub! So one day, we're in chow line, just him and me, and I go up and whisper, so he has to lean close to hear me, "I am going to kill you."

He shouts, "What did you say?"

I speak even softer the second time: "You heard me, Harley. One day, I am going to find you in town, when you're alone, and I am going to kill you."

He goes nuts. "Who the hell do you think you are, Jew boy? You can't talk to me like that." He hits me across the mouth. I wipe away the blood and look up smiling. "Now I've got you, you son of a bitch. You're screwed." I went to the colonel and filed a complaint. Harley was gone. There are all kinds of ways to deal with an adversary: fists, words, taunts, compromise, submission, complaint, and courts-martial.

On one occasion, a service buddy, knowing I was far from home, invited me to his house for the weekend. We got in late Friday and went right to sleep. When we came down to the kitchen Saturday morning, there, sitting at the table, eating his breakfast, was my friend's father dressed in a white robe with a Klan hood next to him in a chair. I kid you not, this actually happened. I sit down, nervous, smiling. He shakes my hand, asks my name, then says, "Weintraub? What kind of name is Weintraub?"

"It's a Jewish name, sir."

"You a Jew?" he says. "No, you no Jew. If you a Jew, where's your horns?"

"Oh, they're there," I tell him. "Just had to file 'em down to fit under the helmet."

I got one of the bleakest postings in the Air Force—Fairbanks, Alaska. It was the wild frontier: dirt streets, trading posts, a saloon with the sort of long wood bar you see in old westerns. Soldiers and contractors stopped in town on their way to the Aleutian Islands, where we had radar stations and listening posts. It was as close as you could get to the Soviet Union without leaving American soil. These men were stationed on the islands for long stretches, did not see a woman for months, did not see the sun for just as long. When they returned to Fairbanks, they picked up their pay in a lump sum, then went on a spree. Aside from soldiers, the town was just bartenders and hookers, both in pursuit of the same mission: separate the doughboys from their cash. I learned a lot in Alaska. In the control tower, I learned how to read coordinates and communicate in code, which, even now, as I'm trying to sleep, comes back in maddening bursts of dots and dashes. In the barracks, where I ran a floating craps game—it appeared and disappeared like the blips on the radar screen—I learned the tricks of procurement. In town, I learned how to move product.

One day, I spotted a beautiful coat in the window of the Sachs Men's Shop in Fairbanks. (Note the spelling: S-A-C-H-S.) It was called a Cricketer. (I always had a weakness for clothes.) It was different from the James Dean jacket. It was a sports coat, tweedy and sharp. I went in, stood in the showroom at top of the world, tried on the coat, looked in the mirror. The owner came over, gave me the pitch.

"Yes, I know, I know, but how much?"

"Twenty dollars."

"Sorry, out of my league. I'm an enlisted man."

"Well, how much have you got?"

"Three dollars."

"Okay, how about you give me your three dollars and we do the rest on modified consignment. Give me two dollars a week. That way, you can enjoy the jacket as you're paying for it."

"All right."

As he's writing up the ticket, he asks, "What's you're name?"

"Jerry Weintraub."

He looks up, surprised. "Jewish?"

"Yeah."

"Where are you from?"

"New York."

"Hey, me, too!"

He thinks, then says: "Why don't you come here and help out when you're not on duty?"

That's how I ended up working full-time at the Sachs Men's Shop while serving full-time in the Air Force. Between the military pay, the dice game, and the new gig, I was starting to make real money. Selling clothes was okay, of course, but I was ambitious. I wanted to get something bigger going. It was just as it had been with my delivery business: Once I saw the money, I could not stop seeing the money.

Now, as I said, every few days, another crew of guys shipped in from the Aleutian Islands, picked up their checks, and went on a spree. So when these guys, chilled to the bone, holding their cash, came into the street, what's the first thing they saw? The

Sachs Men's Shop. I decided to tell a story, to package a fantasy right in the big front window. I made a beach scene there, with a guy in a bathing suit sitting beside a gorgeous girl, drinking rum under an umbrella as waves break. The men stood there, mesmerized. Then they came in and talked to me. I took some of their money and in return set them up with a whole package, the plane tickets, the Florida hotel, the clothes, the beach stuff—everything but the girl. It was the Star of Ardaban all over again.

By the time of my discharge, I was running the show. I was not sure I would ever again have such a firm handle on things. Mr. Sachs asked me to stay on as a civilian, but this made me laugh. I was anxious to get back. This much I knew: As soon as you feel comfortable, that's when it's time to start over.

Because I Wouldn't Wear Tights

When I got back from the service in 1956, the Bronx had changed. Everyone was seventeen when I went away, in varsity jackets and white bucks, hair slicked into ducktails, on the corner into the night, nothing but time to argue and boast. Everyone was twenty when I returned, and ready to get on with their lives. I wandered the streets in my Cricketer coat, hands in pockets, looking into windows. The corners were empty, my friends were gone. You go away believing that when you return, your world, your house, your parents—all of it will be waiting for you when you get back. But time passes, and you change, and as you change, everything else changes, too, so when you return you realize there is no home to return to. It's gone. When you stood at the train station, waving goodbye, you did not understand what you were waving good-bye to—the world of your childhood dissolved behind you. Maybe it's better that way. If you knew how time works, you would never do anything.

One morning, my father asked me to meet him at his office. He wanted to have a talk. I'm not sure I've said enough about my father. He was a wonderful, sophisticated man, who crossed the world with nothing but a jewel case and his mind. He built a business, supported a family, taught us right from wrong. He was the greatest man I have ever known. I sometimes think his generation accomplished feats that later generations could never match. They carried their families through the Depression and the war, instilled hope in even the worst times, took terrific knocks but went on. But my father was a product of his era and many of his ideas were traditional. There was a way to do things, and a way to live. A man should, for example, build a business, which he can pass on to his sons. He should have a paycheck, a regular source of income, and, most important, he should have an inventory. Inventory—the word rang like a bell in our house. It was magic. A man should be able to go into his storeroom and count his stock. Here is something he told me: At the end of the day, write down exactly what you have. Put that number in your left pocket. Then write down exactly what you owe. Put that number in your right pocket. As long as the number in your left pocket is bigger than the number in your right pocket, you will have a good life.

We met downtown. He was in his forties, glowing with life. He had a special expression on his face, a sweet smile. He said, "Sit." There was a leather case on a chair next to him. It was black and monogrammed with the letters J. W.

"What's that?" I asked.

He put a hand on the bag. "This is your sample case," he told me, "for when you go on the road and sell jewelry."

The blood rushed to my face, the hair on my neck stood up. This monogrammed case—it was like seeing my own coffin. I stuttered and stammered. I said, "No, no, no. I can't. I just can't. That's not what I am going to do. I can't."

He seemed genuinely surprised, shocked. "What do you

mean? You're my son. You are supposed to come into the business, learn it, carry it on. That's how it works."

"That's how what works?"

"The world—that's how the world works."

"No, not my world."

"What are you talking about?" he said. "It's a wonderful business. You will be able to pay your rent, buy a house, feed your family when you have a family."

"Don't worry," I told him, "I'm going to be able to pay the rent and support my family."

"How?"

"I don't know yet."

"What are you going to do?"

"I don't know, but whatever I do, I will do it well, the way you taught me to do everything."

It might sound like a sad scene, in which a father tries to pass a tradition on to his son and his son turns away, but it was not like that at all. It was joyful. I respected and loved my father, but I did not want to live his life—and he understood that, and let me go, and, in a sense, in going my own way, I was actually following his example, which was to find my own way, freestyle, packaging and selling my own Star of Ardaban, checking the number in the right pocket against the number in the left.

I decided I should go back to school, but I was not sure what kind of school. I looked over the list of colleges covered by the GI Bill. Cornell, Haverford, Colgate. I could not picture myself carrying a philosophy text across some leafy campus. I had trained in the South, stood up to bullies, had breakfast with a member of the Klan, sold suits in the tundra—I was just not ready for that kind of college. I decided to audition for the Neighborhood Playhouse School instead. This was one of the acting schools that taught the Method pioneered by Konstantin Stanislavsky, wherein you don't pretend to be a character so much as become that character. In the age of Marlon Brando, everyone wanted to slouch his shoulders and mumble, "Not my night? Oh, Charlie. I could've taken that bum with one hand tied behind my back." I chose the Playhouse because, yes, I liked acting, I loved attention and being on stage, but also because I figured the Playhouse was an ideal spot to meet girls—all those hopefuls fresh from the suburbs and farms of America with dreams of making it on Broadway.

The school was on West Fifty-fourth Street, in midtown Manhattan. It was run by Sandy Meisner, the legendary acting teacher. I went up a flight of stairs, gave my name, and just like that was alone on stage for a tryout, with light pouring down, being studied by Mr. Meisner and his assistant Sydney Pollack, who would later become a great friend of mine. I read some lines, acted some scenes, threw my arms around and shouted, a street kid from the Bronx spewing dialogue from one of those great midcentury plays about the nobility of suffering.

Mr. Meisner stopped me in the middle of my monologue.

"What the hell are you doing?" he asked.

"What do you mean? I'm auditioning."

"Yeah, but you're no actor."

I just stared at him.

"Okay," he said, "walk across the stage."

I walked across the stage.

"I like how you walk," he said. "You walk like John Wayne. But you're still no actor."

"Yeah," I said, "but maybe I will be."

He whispered back and forth with Sydney Pollack, then

said, "Okay, you're a big, good-looking kid. Maybe you're right. Maybe you will be. You're in."

I had moved out of the Bronx by then, and was living with two hookers above P. J. Clarke's on Third Avenue. I had met them one night when everyone was drinking and the air was filled with smoke. I followed them home. I started having an affair with one of them, and they moved me in. I was in class most of the time anyway. The school was a powerhouse, packed with talent. James Caan, Dabney Coleman, Brenda Vaccaro, Elizabeth Ashley—they were all at the school around this time. I remember doing an improvisation with James Caan, the two of us getting so mixed up between the real and the make believe that we came to blows on stage. It ended with me sitting on him, shouting, "I'll kill you, I'll kill you!"

I was not going to be a movie star, that much was clear. I did not have the passion for it, or the talent. "You're no actor." Well, Mr. Meisner was right. In my life, I have only been comfortable playing one role: Jerry Weintraub. Still, I had not made the wrong decision. I learned things at the Playhouse School that have been invaluable. About actors and artists for one, what drives them, what terrifies them (this is often the same as what drives them), what they need. (Managing talent is my business, after all.) These are people who do not make a product, perform an essential service, or, as my father would say, have an inventory, so even the most successful of them are haunted by the following thought: "Who really needs what I'm making?"

If you go to a movie set a week before wrap, you will see the biggest stars in the world on the phone in a panic. "What do I do next?" "Who wants me?" It's not that these people are unusual—it's the situation that's unusual. The on-again, off-again nature of the work would test anyone.

So what do I do? I help. I take the pressure off. I handle the mundane concerns so the actor or director or writer can do what only he or she can do: perform, create. An artist who attempts to get into business—to do what I do, produce or deal or whatever—is an artist who has stopped being an artist. Most important, I do not treat artists like children. I do not patronize. Some people on the business side of entertainment do patronize. They feed off the insecurity of the situation: Your fear is money in their wallet. These are sharks. But other people help artists through that bad stretch after they have finished and before they have started again—these are the David O. Selznicks and Bryan Lourds, the producers and agents who built Hollywood.

I learned a lot from the improv exercises, too. For me, this was less a matter of becoming another person or character than learning to trust the logic of my own mind. Sometimes, when you're up against it, maybe this is an old Bronx thing, you just have to open your mouth and start talking. I can't tell you how many jams I've gotten out of by talking, seeing where the words take me. "What are we going to do about it?" "Well, I'll tell you what we're going to do about it…" And I open my mouth and see what happens. That's improv.

For me, the end of the Playhouse School came during dance class—or, to be more specific, when Jimmy Caan and I went to buy clothes for dance class. This was Martha Graham's workshop. It was legendary—every student had to take it. Jimmy's father drove a fruit truck and took us to Capezio on Broadway in that truck. We get out—and we were street kids, you'd never peg us in a million years for actors—and go up to the showroom where they sell the clothes. A saleswoman puts a tape measure around my waist, chest, shoulders, then comes back with a stack of stuff, slippers, tights, whatever. I put it on and look at myself in the mirror, and I'm like, "Whoa! Wait a minute. If I walked down the street in my neighborhood like this, they'd kill me." And here's the kicker: They would be right to kill me! I would deserve killing! So I look at Jimmy, and say, "Nope. Uh-uh. Can't do it. No way."

I go to the class in my jeans and T-shirt. I'm surrounded by dancers, these beautiful butterflies. I never felt so big in my life. I was Sylvester Stallone trapped in a painting by Edgar Degas. Martha Graham comes out, elegant, floating around, and says, "Where are our tights and dancing slippers?"

I shrug and say, "I can't wear that stuff."

"In my class," she says, "you wear my clothes."

"Look at me," I tell her. "I'm never going to be a dancer. I don't want to buy the clothes."

She puts her hand to her chin and cocks her hip and sighs. "Okay. Let me see you walk."

Now, by walk she did not mean walk. She meant ballet walk. Up on your toes. When I get across the room, turn, and look, she throws up her hands and says, "You, sir, are a klutz!"

This was the dividing line, the moment of truth. Jimmy Caan put on the slippers and tights, so his name appears in the credits as Sonny Corleone or whatever, whereas I, being filled with normal human shame, did not put on the slippers and tights, so my name appears in various credits as producer.

Years later, I produced *Martha Graham on Broadway*. Did she remember me from class? Of course not. It's opening night. I sent her ten dozen roses, filled her dressing room with flowers, then showed up in my tuxedo, doing the whole F. Scott Fitzgerald routine, walking through the lobby, smiling and waving. A girl grabbed me by the cuff. "Ms. Graham wants to see you right away." I went to her dressing room, knocked. She threw open the door with a flourish. She was tiny but had huge gestures, was very dramatic. She took me by the wrists, pulled me close, and said, "You sir, are my impresario! My impresario, oh, my impresario! The greatest impresario in the world!"

"No," I told her," "I'm not your impresario. I'm your klutz."

Stay Off the WATS Line

I began to look for work a few months after I started taking classes. The business side of entertainment—that's where I was heading as far back as the family trip to the Fox lot. I applied to all the television networks and talent agencies in the city, intern, gofer, office boy, mailroom clerk, anything to get in the door. Most of the big outfits had unofficial programs to recruit executive talent. The men who hired for these jobs—it was always men—were middle-aged midlevel executives. I had an ability to win over these men and land myself these jobs. I was first hired as a page at NBC, this being, for many, the first step in a corporate program that turned the raw-boned kid into the executive in a Brooks Brothers suit.

There were hardly any Jews in the page program—it was mostly Irish kids. I remember the jacket they gave you the first day: a gorgeous blue coat, a gold braid snaking down the lapel.

I worked at the Hudson Theater on Forty-fourth Street, where I later produced *Ann Corio, This Is Burlesque*, and made a fortune. I lined up crowds, ushered people into their seats. *The Steve Allen Show, The Jerry Lester Show, Broadway Tonight with Dagmar*, I worked on them all. I was in and out of the theater all day, talking, schmoozing, picking up bits of gossip. I met Sophie Tucker. I met Ted Lewis. I met Steve Allen. I met Jerry Lester. I met Dagmar, a beautiful woman. I was getting an incredible look at an era that was vanishing: the Golden Age of Television. It was the late fifties. Ten years later, all these shows would be gone. It taught me about the rise and fall of empires, the fickle nature of fame. The point is, do not get attached to the world as it is, because the world is changing, something new is coming, every ten years a big hand comes down and sweeps the dishes off the table.

I have many memories from this time: running down West Forty-third Street in the rain to get a bottle of scotch for Sophie Tucker; smoking a cigarette with Steve Allen before his show; talking to Dagmar, who was certain her career would soon be over; taking a few bucks to seat some sailor boys in the *Tonight Show* audience at the last minute (tickets were free), walking them across a clean white stage, their boots leaving muddy black prints, the producer losing his mind (thought I would get fired for that one). But mostly, I remember how it felt to be young and in the city with my whole life in front of me. I stood watching the crowd, my mind cool and sharp, my hands at my sides, but another part of me was not cool and sharp, but fiery and excited. It was powerful, the happiness that rose in my chest and roared in my ears like the engine of a car when you step on the gas with the gearshift in neutral.

I knew I would not stay long in the page program, or climb the ladder to the executive suite. I would stay until I got what I needed, then move on. Various jobs, that's what interested me. That could be my coda. Various experiences, various adventures.

Within a year of starting at NBC, I traded my blue coat and golden braid for a blue blazer. I was now working in the mailroom of the William Morris Agency. It was a grind. I was there early and stayed late, reading and sorting mail, delivering packages and studying the politics of the place. Grunt jobs are often the most instructive—they allow you to flow through an organization unnoticed, a corpuscle or cell moving in and out of the heart and lungs. William Morris was probably the most storied talent agency in New York, founded in the 1800s, when its hottest clients had been magicians, escape artists, song and dance men. Its mailroom was legendary, known in the business as *the mailroom*, a breeding ground for the future business talent of Hollywood. Michael Eisner, Bernie Brillstein—they all came through the William Morris mailroom, a credential worn in Hollywood as some wear the Legion of Honor.

I'm always hearing from people who say they worked with me in the mailroom at William Morris, but the odds are slim—I was only there for two months.

One afternoon, I went to lunch at the Park Central Hotel on Sixth Avenue. It was a notorious spot. Arnold Rothstein, the father of the Jewish underworld, had been shot in a room in the hotel, and Albert Anastasia, the boss of Murder Incorporated, had been shot in the barbershop off the lobby. It was a showbiz hangout, a haunt of managers and agents. I sat alone in the corner. Two young executives were at the next table talking in voices you could not help but overhear about a job that had just opened at MCA, the talent agency run by Jules Stein and Lew Wasserman. Their conversation was detailed and specific. One of the men said the posting was in the TV department, and that the man hiring was named Dick Rubin.

I finished my meal, went back to the mailroom, and called

Dick Rubin. When his secretary answered, I said, in the coolest voice possible, "It's Jerry Weintraub for Dick Rubin." A minute later, when Rubin got on, I said, "Dick, Jerry Weintraub. I hear you're looking for someone in TV. Well, I am over here at William Morris and none too happy."

I went for an interview the following afternoon. MCA—Music Corporation of America—was a talent agency founded in the 1920s by Jules Stein. Lew Wasserman, who grew up in Cleveland, Ohio, and started, like I did, as an usher in a movie theater, joined the company in the 1940s. He spent years in the trenches, working his way up. By the time of my interview, he was living and working in LA, but you could still feel his presence in the New York office. It was Wasserman's company.

Dick Rubin was surprised by how young I was. I had really played it up on the phone, giving him the impression, probably, that I was an agent—not a kid from the mailroom. But I have a skill for interviews, and I got the job. Just like that, I went from making twenty-five dollars a week to making over seventy-five. My immediate boss was a big-time TV executive named Hubbell Robinson. He produced a bunch of shows, including the *Ford Theatre*, which was very prestigious. I was called Robinson's assistant, but was really a glorified secretary. I sat at a desk outside his office, fetched coffee, ran errands. In the interview, he asked me a bunch of questions, like "Can you type?" and "Can you take dictation?" and "Do you know shorthand?"

"Oh, yes, sure, absolutely"—of course, I could do none of that stuff.

In the first weeks, whenever Robinson asked me to type something, I would get one of the girls in the secretarial pool to do it for me. If he dictated a letter, I would listen carefully, run out, and dictate whatever I could remember to one of the girls. This worked for a time. Then, one day, Robinson asked me to take down what he described as a "very important letter." I went into his office with my pad and pencil, crossed my legs, assumed the position. He cleared his throat, then started: "Dear Mr. Muckety Muck, re: the matter of December 4 blah, blah, blah…" I followed as best as I could, but was soon left behind. He talked for two or three minutes—a long time—then said, "Okay, Jerry, read it back."

I sat up, turned over the page, and started, "Dear Mr. Muckety Muck, re: the matter of December 4," stumbled, stammered, then said, "Well, after that was something about a contract, or a litigant, or an out-of-country actor…?"

He looked at me like, you know, what the heck? then said, "Do you know shorthand, Jerry?"

"No."

"Can you type?"

"No."

"What did you think would happen when you got in here and sat down, and I started giving you this letter?"

"I don't know," I said. "I guess I was hoping it would just come to me, that I would suddenly know how to do it. I've heard of even crazier things happening."

He asked me to leave. There were meetings and discussions. After lunch, I was called back into Mr. Robinson's office. He said, "Look, Jerry, we're not going to fire you. We like you—we like having you around. We think you're going to be great. But stop trying to take dictation and stop trying to type. We'll get an assistant for that. We're promoting you to junior agent."

What lesson do I take?

Be willing to be lucky.

Look at me. I had stumbled from chance to chance, emerging

each time not only intact but with a better title and a bigger salary. I was one of the suit-wearing agents of MCA now, with clients of my own, making a hundred dollars a week. But I think it was more than luck. I think I was being tested, as everyone is tested in this business, the object being—even if the bosses don't mean it consciously—to see who can think on his or her feet, who can survive. The job of an agent is, in part, anyway, to bullshit and schmooze: How better to find talent than by seeing who can talk his way into a career? From usher to mailroom to secretarial pool to my own office.

It was like falling up a flight of stairs.

I had gotten back together with my high-school sweetheart—the girl who sent me the care packages in Biloxi. She was working as a secretary in the LA office of MCA. I called her every few nights on the WATS line, a party line that kept the East Coast and West Coast offices of the company in contact. You dialed Canal 6-0083-212 and a second later an operator picked up: "MCA, Beverly Hills."

So one night I am at my desk in New York, feet up—I always did have excellent taste in shoes—talking to my future ex-wife, and we get into one those awful screaming fights you only have when you're a kid. Five minutes later, you can't even remember what it was about.

I come to work the next morning, seven, seven-thirty. I was usually the first one in. I sit down, and, before I can take a sip of my coffee, the phone rings. It's the switchboard. "Is this Jerry Weintraub?"

"Yes."

"Please clear your lines. Lew Wasserman is calling."

I had never met Lew Wasserman. I mean, he was the president of the company, the voice speaking from the burning bush, and I was a pissy junior agent.

I did the math. Seven-thirty in New York. Making it . . . six-thirty, five-thirty . . . For the love of God, why is the president of the company calling me at four-thirty in the morning?

I wait, listening to the static on the line, to the beating of my own heart, then he comes on—big, booming voice.

"Is this Mr. Weintraub?"

"Yes, sir."

"What department are you in, Mr. Weintraub?"

He was showing me that he knew I was a peanut.

"Commercials."

"Were you on the WATS line last night with your girlfriend, Mr. Weintraub?"

"Yes."

"Do you know for how long?"

"Well, no, but it seemed like forever."

"It was three hours and twelve minutes, Mr. Weintraub. Did you enjoy your conversation?"

"No, not particularly."

"Well, I listened to some of it and it was terrible. How can you talk like that?"

"You listened to my conversation?"

"I wanted to reach Mr. Stein in New York, and was trying to get on the WATS line, but they told me it was being tied up by a Mr. Weintraub."

Wasserman had probably expected me to obfuscate, bullshit, stammer, or lie, but I instead told the truth. Which disarmed him immediately and made it so he would probably never forget me. *I mean, can you believe this kid?*

There was a pause, then he said, "When I come to New York, I want to meet you."

A few weeks later, he called, asked me to his office. We talked, and later talked again, then again, and gradually, over time, we became friends.

By the early sixties, MCA represented the biggest names in Hollywood. The agency had a kind of monopoly on star power, which allowed Wasserman to go to the studio bosses, who had always enjoyed total control, and say, "Look, you have a choice: Either you share some of that control, or you make your films without our stars." In this way, he was able to negotiate for his clients an unheard-of degree of freedom, meaning they could choose their projects, move from studio to studio, let the market determine their fees, which meant a shift of power from management to talent and, ultimately, the breakup of the old system. Of course, this all came back to bite Wasserman later, when he turned MCA into a studio.

I learned a lot from Lew: from his rise, from how he built his agency and studio, but also from his limitations, which resulted from the very quality that made him a success—his sympathy and identification with talent. He operated close to the ground, among the actors and directors who were turning out the product, thus sometimes missed the big picture—the tracking shot—which was, after all, part of his job. The vision thing. I think that's why MCA was later taken over by Matsushita, by Seagrams. Simply put, Wasserman missed a turn in the plot. The other studios launched television networks, theme parks, diversified and grew, but did Wasserman develop an HBO or MTV? No. Sony, Paramount, Disney, Columbia—they all realized they had to get bigger to survive, but Wasserman kept MCA small. Big but small. When the game changes, you have to change with it. The more you change, the more you risk in order to survive—and it gets harder and scarier as you get older.

Not long after our first meeting, Wasserman gave me a shot. He moved me up and let me float, meaning I worked all over the company, in every department, which was a great opportunity. Why did he do this for me? Because, when the obvious thing was to lie (about the WATS line) I told the truth. That was unusual. It set me apart. It made me interesting, and interesting is valuable. I was now in a position to see how the company really worked, how the deals were really made, how a contract was negotiated, how the terms were reached, how the points were traded and the deal closed, but—here is the funny part—the more I observed, the more I realized how much I knew already. I already instinctively knew how to handle a client, how to deal with a demand, how to back off a bully, how to make everyone walk away feeling good about how bad the other guy was feeling—this was pure Bronx, street-corner stuff.

After a few years working for Wasserman, I felt I had learned all that I was going to learn and was ready to move on. Maybe it was that old restlessness again. I was tired of being a cog in another man's machine. It might seem strange to walk away from such a plum gig, a risk, but I did not feel like I was taking a risk. I was just doing what I had always done. It did not matter if it was Lew Wasserman or my father with his jewelry case. I did not want to follow another man's script. I was living my own plot, following my own light. How did I know it was time to move on? How do you know that a movie is over? The girl kisses the boy, the credits roll, you stand up and leave. I was twenty-four. I had decided to start my own business.

I told Lew I was leaving. We were in his office in New York. He came around the desk, took off his glasses. "You're doing what?"

"I'm leaving."

It was exhilarating—not quitting Lew, because I loved Lew, but taking control of my life and my career, choosing, saying, "I want to do this, not that."

That's freedom—that's all it really is.

He put his hand on my shoulder.

He said, "This is a mistake."

He said, "This is the best possible place for you."

He said, "Do you understand what kind of opportunity I have given you?"

Finally, when he saw my mind was made up, he went back around his desk, sat down, and said, "When you leave here, where do you think you're going?"

I said, "I don't know."

He said, "You mean to say you're going to quit MCA, and you don't even know where you're going?"

"Yes."

He said, "You're not as smart as I thought you were, Jerry."

Years later, after I had bought a house just up the street from Lew, some representatives of a fund-raising group came to see me. They said they wanted to honor me, throw me a dinner, blah, blah. They were flowery in their rhetoric as to me, but as you get older you come to understand the real reason you're chosen for such honors: because the committee of whatever thinks your name can sell tables. It's not you they are after, in other words, it's your address book. Five or six of them sat in the living room, explaining why I had been selected. *It's you and only you, Mr. Weintraub; you are the only man who is worthy.* I finally interrupted them, saying, "Look, there is another man far more deserving than me living just down the street. In fact, I would feel uncomfortable receiving such an honor with him unhonored."

They moved to the edge of the couch.

One of them asked, "Yes, yes? Who is it?"

"Just go three houses in that direction and ask for Lew Wasserman," I told them.

"But we already offered it to him," the man said. "It was Mr. Wasserman who sent us here."

Being P. T. Barnum

In the spring of 1961, I married my high-school sweetheart. We had been a classic neighborhood couple. I was a football player, she was a cheerleader. We got married because getting married is what you did. We were young, inexperienced. We fought all the time, banged off each other like molecules in a vial. The breakup was my fault. I was a bad husband. I don't call it a mistake, because our son Michael, who is wonderful, my best friend in the world, came out of that marriage. He stayed with her in New York when I moved to LA. I think a lot of bad things were said about me, which, of course, only made him more curious to know his father. When he was twelve, he said he wanted to move to California and live with me. It was Michael's choice, but it upset my ex-wife terribly. I don't think she's ever gotten over it. And I totally understand that.

The marriage lasted just a few years. We lived on Saunders Street, in Rego Park, Queens. I was just starting my business, which meant I was insane with work. Hustling. The company was called Directional Enterprises. I had an office in a part of Midtown then dominated by show business types. The lobby was filled with small-time producers and writers and actors and various other hangers-on. In the beginning, I would take on anyone who happened through my door. I was always ready to make the small thing big, or the big thing huge. (A talent manager must be an optimist.) Animal acts, magicians, hypnotists, conjurers, saloon singers, dancers—I represented them all. Woody Allen had an office in the same building. He would ride the elevator with me and my clients—the juggler, for example—and overhear me saying things like, "We're going to build an event around you! You're not just a juggler, but an artist! Do you hear me? An artist!" I often wondered if Woody based *Broadway Danny Rose* on me and my more marginal acts.

I heard Paul Anka before he was Paul Anka—even then, he was a star—working on his great early hit "Diana." I signed four kids from New Jersey: Frankie Valli, Bob Gaudio, Tommy DeVito, and Nick Massi, who called themselves the "Four Seasons." We went on a ballroom tour, the five of us—me being the Fifth Season—eating and sleeping in the van. We reached Chicago exhausted and starved. The manager of the ballroom, an old Chicagoan, said, "You guys are a mess, go next door, have a steak, a cocktail, my treat." "Sherry," which became the group's big hit, had just been released, and when we got back, the house was packed. We were supposed to get a percentage of the gate. "This is great," I told the manager. "Our first sellout!"

"Sellout?" He said, "Nah, no one was coming, so I just let these people in for free."

It was a crucial early lesson: Buy your own steak; it's cheaper.

On most nights, I was out till dawn, racing through Manhattan from club to club, scouting, booking, signing acts. I used to sit with Barbara Walters in back of the Latin Quarter, a famous Broadway hot spot owned by her father, Lou Walters. "Hey, Barbara, who's been filling the seats?" I'd ask her. I was in search of established acts, but was also trying to hit on the right package or trick to sell tickets. I have never been afraid to try even the craziest idea. Later on, I would sell Elvis tickets by advertising: "On sale Monday morning, 9:00 A.M., first come, first served." What does that even mean? Of course the first one gets served first. But I made headlines out of that. And everything I did was a limited edition. But what are they limited to? 82 million? 700 million? 455 million? I mean, there's no law about it. I think this is why I got along better with older men than with my contemporaries. When I told my ideas to people my age, they would wave me away, call me nutty. But when I brought these same ideas to people who had been around, such as Colonel Tom Parker or Frank Sinatra, they got it right away. They knew just who I was and just what I wanted to be. Not a junior agent, not a young man on a ladder to the executive suite, but P. T. Barnum!

I'll give you an example.

Around 1963, I had an idea drifting through my head. I wanted to put on a softball game at Yankee Stadium, in which Elvis would captain a team against a team captained by Ricky Nelson. I had booked Ricky Nelson at the Steel Pier in Atlantic City, but did not know anyone with the Yankees, or anyone with Elvis. I just figured the idea would generate the relationships. I called Dan Topping, who owned the Yankees. It took some persistence, but he finally agreed to meet me. We met in his office at the stadium. I said, "Mr. Topping, I want to rent your facility."

At first, he thought I was crazy. In those days, no one rented out stadiums. But when I made the pitch, his tone changed. "That's pretty interesting," he said. "Do you actually know Elvis Presley?"

"No," I said, "not yet."

"And besides, what makes you think that tens of thousands of people will pay to watch Elvis play softball? Do you understand how big this place is?"

"Sure," I told him. "I've been scalping your box seats for years."

"Come with me," he said, "I want to show you something."

He brought me down the ramp and out onto the field, then stood me at second base. "Look around," he said.

Have you ever stood in an empty baseball stadium? It's unbelievable, all those seats, each representing a person who has to be reached, marketed to, convinced, sold. It was intimidating, and it stayed with me. Whenever I am considering an idea, I picture the seats rising from second base at Yankee Stadium. Can I sell that many tickets? Half that many? Twice that many? In the end, the softball game did not come off, but neither did Dan Topping think I was crazy. An idea is only crazy, after all, until someone pulls it off.

Within a year or two, Directional Enterprises was putting on shows all across the country. I had a hit at the Brooklyn Paramount, a fantastic theater. One night, after curtain, two guys come in, big guys in flashy suits. One of them steps forward, the talker, you know the type. *This is how it's gonna be, this is what you're gonna do.* "From now on," he says, "me, you, and him is partners."

I consider, sort of confused, then say, "But I don't want partners."

"You don't understand," he tells me. "You're in Brooklyn. Brooklyn is our neighborhood. We get a piece of whatever happens in our neighborhood. So we're now partners."

I was tough, but not stupid tough, and now I was scared.

"Ask around," the man says, "find out who we are, and we'll be back tomorrow to work out the this and that."

I raced home in a panic and called my father. He had been around; he knew and had dealt with tough guys before. He grew up in the Bronx, after all, where if you were in business, there was really no avoiding the underworld. He had met Abe Reles and Meyer Lansky—all the players in the Jewish mob. He said, "Jerry, Jerry, take a breath. Calm down. It's okay. It's the way of the world."

"What do I do?" I asked.

"Tell me the story," he said. "Slowly, all the details. I want to see if I can figure out who these guys might be."

When I finished, he said, "Okay. Let me talk to somebody. You'll hear from me soon."

An hour later, he called back and said, "You are to be at [such and such a bar] on the Upper East Side tomorrow at 9:00 P.M., where you will meet a man. Talk to him. He will help you."

"Who is he?" I asked.

"Just see him."

"Okay."

"And Jerry."

"Yeah?"

"Don't be late. If you piss him off, it's not an angry letter he's going to send."

The next night, I went to the club on the East Side, a strip bar on First Avenue right out of *The Sopranos*. Someone took me to a room in back, where I was introduced to the man my father had told me about. He was the boss of one of the New York crime families. He was a tough man—I mean, you would not mess with him—but he had a code, and he played by that code, and he had an air of nobility. He was alone at his table, with a plate of food and a bottle of wine. The room was filled with his lieutenants. He said, "Sit." He had a size twenty-two neck and a giant head, like a head on an old Roman bust. He was huge—it was like someone came in every few hours and injected him with pasta. But he had a face, this great, kind, very human face, and I liked him immediately. I was scared, but I liked him. He poured me a glass of wine and said, "So tell me, what's the problem?"

"Well, these two guys came to see me in Brooklyn where I have a show going and they told me they're going to be my partners."

"Yes, so?"

"I don't want partners."

"But it's their neighborhood," said the boss. "You're taking money out of their store—you gotta give them a percentage."

"I don't want to."

"You don't want to? Why not?"

"Because I don't want to be involved in anything illegal," I said. "I pay my taxes. I just want to make my money and live my life."

He sat there for a moment, thinking, then said, "Here's what we're going to do. I'm going to tell these guys not to bother you. But, in return, you have to promise me something: You're never going to do anything illegal. In your whole life. What the world considers illegal."

He said this slowly, deliberately, letting the words sink in. He was a bright guy. I think he graduated from Fordham.

I said okay.

"No," he told me. "You have to promise it. You will never get involved with anything illegal inside or outside this country, because if you do, I'm coming back and taking a piece of everything you have."

"Okay," I said. "I promise."

"You're sure that's what you want?" he asked.

"Yes."

"You know, Jerry, you could make a lot of money doing stuff with us."

"Well, I want to see if I can make a lot of money doing stuff without you."

He looked at me, sizing me up, then said, "I want you here tomorrow at seven o'clock."

I went back the next night, drank with the boss, then the guys came in. The boss sat them down and said, "Let me explain something to you two. Jerry is now my nephew. He is under my protection. Nobody touches him. Nobody gets near him. In fact, if anything happens to him while he's in Brooklyn, you two guys are responsible."

After that, I could not go to the bathroom in Brooklyn without these two guys following to make sure I did not trip and bang my head on the toilet.

Even after the show closed, I continued to stop by the club on the East Side to say hello to the boss. We started a friendship that lasted the rest of our lives. He flew to Beverly Hills for my son Michael's Bar Mitzvah. The boss is still around. He's an old man now, but is still being watched by the FBI.

Sometime in the late 1970s, I had a conversation with Steve Ross, the chairman of Warner Bros. He wanted me to put in some money so we could buy the Westchester Premier Theatre, which was near his house. By then I had long worked with Sinatra and Elvis, and many others, so it made sense. We could fill it up with top-drawer entertainment. "Beautiful," I said, "start writing the papers." A few days later, I get a call. It's the boss. He says, "Meet me at the Grotto. We need to talk." He meant the Grotto Azura, one of the oldest restaurants in Little Italy.

We sat in the main room, the boss with his back to the wall.

He said, "Jerry, you broke your promise."

"What promise?" I asked.

"Remember," he said, "you promised you would never get involved with anything illegal."

"Yeah," I said, "but I kept that promise."

"No, you haven't," he said. "You're buying the Westchester Premier Theatre, aren't you?"

"Yes."

"Well, who do you think owns the Westchester Premier Theatre? We do, through waste management. We have the garbage contract. And we have seats there we don't manifest. That's illegal. And I'm not getting out of the theater just because you're buying. Which means you will be involved in something the world considers illegal."

"Oh, shit," I said. "What should I do?"

"Don't buy it."

The next morning, I called Steve Ross and told him, "I'm not buying into this theater, and neither should you."

When I told him why, he dismissed me, saying, "Oh, come on, don't be ridiculous."

So I didn't buy into the theater, and he did, and it gave him a lot of trouble.

Over the years, as I booked acts, I became friends with the guys who ran the resorts in the Catskills, in the Poconos, in Vegas.

Now and then, they would turn their theaters over to me for the thirty or so dead nights that followed New Year's. *Nothing is selling anyway, why not give Jerry a shot?* I would invent shows out of nothing, the wilder the better, parties and extravaganzas, packaged and marketed like mad. It became my trademark: "A Night in Paris," "A Night in London." Nutty stuff, scrap. I had an act I had been trying to break forever: Kimo Lee and the Modernesians, a sword dancer, a singer, and two girls swaying in grass skirts. I had them booked in the Latin Quarter, in New York City, for $750 a week, but wanted to move them to the next level. Then, one day, I get a call from Morris Landsbergh, who sort of ran the Flamingo in Las Vegas. I say sort of because Landsbergh was really just a front for Meyer Lansky. Landsbergh would walk around the casino all day in a blue coat, hair parted, saying, "Hey, how are ya," "Nice to have ya." "Hey, thanks for coming!"

"Jerry, I'm in a jam," Morris tells me. "I need an act for Christmas. What do you got?"

This is the moment: three lemons line up in the slot machine and you wait to see if the fourth will drop.

"How much can you pay?" I ask.

"Fifty thousand dollars a week," says Morris.

Okay. This was real money. At the time, the highest-paid performer in Vegas was the opera singer Mario Lanza, and he was getting fifty a week. Frank Sinatra and those guys were getting twenty-five.

"Oh, sure," I say, "I've got something."

"Well..."

"Well, what...?"

(I'm thinking.)

"What do you have?"

"Well, I will tell you what I have..."

(Still thinking.)

I had been reading James Michener's *Hawaii*. I had never been to Hawaii, but I loved the book. My mind was filled with volcanoes and pigs on spits, shiny dwarf apples shoved between their teeth, and, at the same time, I had this act I was trying to break, so naturally I concoct.

"I have an unbelievable show," I tell Landsbergh. "In fact, it's not just a show. It's an experience. It's called 'A Night in Hawaii.'"

"'A Night in Hawaii'? What the hell is 'A Night in Hawaii'?"

"'A Night in Hawaii,'" I tell him, "is fifty beautiful dancing girls. 'A Night in Hawaii' is waitresses in grass skirts, pigs on spits, the mood of the islands. 'A Night in Hawaii' is a mountain erupting and lava flowing as the music plays!"

"Wow," says Landsbergh. "That sounds like a hell of a show! But as great as it sounds, I don't know if it sounds like a fifty-thousand-dollar show. Now, if you had Arthur Godfrey..."

Arthur Godfrey was one of the first great TV stars. He had two shows on CBS: *Talent Scouts* and *The Arthur Godfrey Hour*. He also had a famous love for Hawaii. He played ukulele and did a whole Pacific islands routine.

"Well, it does!" I tell Landsbergh.

"Does what?"

"Have Arthur Godfrey. In fact, the show is called 'Arthur Godfrey's A Night in Hawaii.'"

"How much?"

"Fifty thousand dollars a week, maybe fifty-five thousand."

"Great! Done! Deal!"

And now I had to get Arthur Godfrey.

I waited until the end of the day, then went down Broadway to the theater where Godfrey taped *Talent Scouts*. There was a security guard with a clipboard and a gun. I have a theory. If you act like you're in charge, no one will stop you. So I go up this guy with a piece of paper in my hand and ask him a bunch of questions—"How long is your present shift?" "Did you find your training adequate to the task?"—say, "Thanks, you're doing a great job," pat him on the shoulder, then walk past him to the elevators. No problem. When I get up to the floor, I wander around until I find a dressing room with Godfrey's name on it. He was one of the biggest stars in the country—you were not supposed to just bang on his door, but, you know, the fourth lemon, the fourth lemon.

Knock, knock, knock.

"Who's there?"

"Jerry Weintraub."

"Oh, yeah, hey, Jerry, come in!"

He probably thought I was the cigar boy.

He was sitting in a chair, napkin around his neck, looking in the mirror, dabbing a pancake pad all over his face. In those days, they all did their own makeup. He was an elegant man with a clean, vanilla way about him. The singer Eddie Fisher said that Godfrey was anti-Semitic. The hotel he partly owned in Miami Beach, the Kenilworth, did not allow Jews. But he was nice to me. "What can I do for you?" he asked.

I said, "Well, Mr. Godfrey, I've come to you with an opportunity to make fifty thousand dollars a week."

"Wow, what is it?"

"It's a show in Las Vegas," I told him. "It's called 'Arthur Godfrey's A Night in Hawaii.'"

"You mean a floor show?" he asks.

"Yeah," I tell him. "In one of the big hotels."

"No, sorry, kid. It's my policy. I don't work live."

"Yeah, but fifty thousand dollars a week," I say. "Maybe more."

"Nope," he says. "Don't work live."

"Yeah, but listen," I say, "you'll be on stage with fifty beautiful Hawaiian girls, and here is the best part: You and I will go to Hawaii and pick them out personally, right off the beach!"

He looks up, like, *Wait, FIFTY Hawaiian girls?* Frowns and says, "Yeah, but it would still be live."

I went on and on, but could not talk him into it. He was scared to death of a live audience. Well, he was then, anyway, because he did call me years later, when his TV career was on the wane, and said, "Jerry, I'm ready to play Vegas. And I want to bring my horse on stage. And I want you to book it." And I did book it, and he did bring his horse on stage.

In the end, I was able to put a show together without Godfrey that worked for Morris Landsbergh. Kimo Lee and the Modernesians, the girls in grass skirts, and the volcano erupting night after night. In other words, the fourth lemon dropped.

Kimo Lee died young. In his will, he left me the rights to a song that had not done much for him. But it was later recorded by Elvis Presley, and after that by just about everyone in the business. It was called "Blue Hawaii."

Fun with Jane

By 1963, I had amassed a stable of talent. There was Kimo Lee and the Modernesians, but also Joey Bishop, Jack Paar, the Four Seasons, and many more. In this business, it only takes one, but who wants to live that way, on a single throw of the dice, or by wrapping yourself in the fortunes of a single artist, no matter how brilliant—the point, as the chaperones used to say at the high-school dance, is to get out there and mix.

I represented two actors Walt Disney wanted for his upcoming *Bon Voyage*, starring Fred MacMurray and Jane Wyman. Mr. Disney flew me to LA first-class, then had a limousine bring me to the Beverly Hills Hotel, where I was set up in a bungalow. I was chauffeured to the Disney Lot, where I was given my own office and a secretary. Five days went by and all they said was, "Mr. Disney is not ready to see you yet." I sat forever. Now and then, my secretary buzzed, asking, "Don't you want to dictate a letter?" "Don't you want to make a call?" (I phoned my mother several times.) Finally, after five days, word came: The maestro was ready. As I remember it, I had to walk down a long hall with Oscars lining the walls on either side. By the time I reached the office at the end, I was intimidated, parched. I felt like I had come through the desert. I shook hands with Mr. Disney, sat down. He was at his desk, drawing, I imagined, a picture of Mickey (him) pounding Goofy (me) with a club. I was, in short, defeated before I heard the opening offer.

Mr. Disney said, "This is what we're going to do."

I said fine.

Mr. Disney said, "This is what your clients are going to get paid."

I said fine.

I learned a lot on this trip: about context, home field advantage, the cost of letting the other side establish its authority. I learned something else, too—about obsession, control. Before I left, I asked Mr. Disney what he was drawing. It was not Mickey hitting Goofy with a club. It was a design for the bathing suit Deborah Walley would wear in *Bon Voyage*. He did not have a costume designer do it. He did it himself. The man was intense, but in an admirable way. He believed he had to control his product, utterly, as the product was really just him in another way. It was a lesson I would learn myself years later, when I started my own production company.

Around this time, an agent and friend from William Morris called. "Jerry," he said, "you should go see Jane Morgan. Her manager died and she needs representation."

I knew Jane Morgan, had heard of her, anyway. She was one of the most talented singers in America. I had seen her on the Jackie Gleason and the Perry Como shows. She was a star. What's more, she had class. Jane Morgan was not Jane's real name, by the way. Her real name was Florence Currier. She grew up in Massachusetts, in an old American family. Her father played in the Boston Symphony. He was first-chair cellist for twenty-five years, which is a big deal. Jane was surrounded by music from the time she was a girl. She trained in opera, but made her name singing the sort of saloon songs that dominated the charts. She broke first in Europe, with hit records and hit shows in all the best clubs, including her regular gig at the Club des Champs Elysées in Paris. She worked with a guy named Bernard Hilda. First it was his name in big letters, with her name in little letters beneath—then it was the opposite. Her American breakthrough came in 1958, with a song called "Fascination." She had a huge career, with hit songs and shows, gigs at supper clubs, more appearances on *The Ed Sullivan Show* than any other singer— when that show was *the* show—and her amazing performance on Broadway in *Mame*. When I was twenty years old, Jane was crooning from every radio.

I went to see her at a theater one night in Pennsylvania. It was raining. The roads were wet. I paid at the door. I sat in back. People around me were talking. She sang in French, her voice sexy and strong. It got in my head and stayed there. She wandered across the stage, lighting up the room as she went. She had short blonde hair and almond-shaped eyes. She owned the crowd, but made the crowd believe they owned her. Whatever an agent looks for but almost never finds, Jane had it. I waited for her backstage. We went outside. The rain came down. We leaned in a doorway. Her hand touched mine. I told her my name. She said my name. I told her my business. My business was helping her business. We sat in a restaurant. We talked about her career. We talked about everything. When I came back to the city—I was always leaving and coming back in those years, the glass towers rising before me—I came back with a relationship that would change my life.

I managed many other clients, but from then on there was really just Jane. I did all the things a manager is supposed to do, booked her shows, negotiated her deals, sat in the audience and in the studio as she cut her records, but what could I really do for her? Of course, I thought I could do a lot. She was a big star. I could make her bigger. But the truth is, in the early years, it was Jane who was helping me. As I've said, my life has been a succession of mentors, but first among these, the person most responsible for making my career, was Jane Morgan. She was married when we met. I was married, too, but, at a certain point, those marriages seemed like nothing compared to what we had together. At that moment, those older relationships just sort of dissolved. We had fallen in love. Jane Morgan, this incredibly successful, beautiful woman whose family came over on the *Mayflower*, and Jerry Weintraub, the kid from the Bronx.

Jane was worldly. She had lived in Paris. She spoke French, Spanish, and Italian. She knew how to go into a restaurant and order a meal. No matter where I went, and no matter what I asked for, I always ended up with a cheeseburger and a Coke. But Jane brought me with her, taught me, broadened my horizons. She took me to Kennebunkport, Maine, where her family lived. She took me to Paris, to Switzerland, all over the world. I went with her on tour. Queens and aristocrats came back after each performance to shake her hand and kiss her cheek. We went to see a Beatles show, early in their career, before anyone knew who they were. They were performing as an opening act for Trini Lopez at the Olympia Theatre in Paris. We went backstage after the show, and they recognized Jane as soon as we came in. They stood up and, in perfect harmony, serenaded her with all her hit songs.

When I was with Jane, I forgot everything else, which is why my first marriage—I was a son of a bitch in that first marriage—stood no chance. I had been knocked down, thrown over. I was dazzled. It was like I had gone from black-and-white to Cinemascope.

Jane divorced her husband, I divorced my wife. It was just me and her after that. She took me everywhere and introduced me to everyone. Frank Sinatra, Tony Bennett, Johnny Carson, Walter Winchell. She had been Miss Dodger. She had been Miss Ebbets Field. Every man in the world wanted to be with her. Howard Hughes and Billy Rose sent gifts, jewelry, flowers, and I signed the ticket. She was an absolute knockout. When we went to a restaurant, we were the restaurant. Or she was the restaurant. I was Mr. Morgan. Which was fine with me. In fact, I took advantage of it. It did wonders for my career. Now, when I came to LA, I did not sit waiting in a bungalow for five days. Joe Pasternak, Arthur Freed, all the great producers, directors, and writers suddenly wanted to meet with me. Jane was the queen. She wore white gloves. I was her manager.

I suppose I'm describing how I built my network, which is a key to my success. A lot depends on who you know, who you can get to. If you have people who will open the door for you, literally and figuratively, you can make a pitch. It's in your hands from there. Soon after I arrived in Hollywood, for example, I struck up a friendship with a guy named Scotty, who worked the gate at the MGM lot. For me, Scotty was more important than Louis B. Mayer. Mr. Mayer might green-light a picture, but you can't get the green light if you can't make the pitch and you can't make the pitch if you can't get in the gate.

One night, in 1965, I turned to Jane, who was getting dolled up for a show at the Flamingo Hotel in Las Vegas, and said, "You know, baby, you look so goddamned beautiful, let's get married!"

She said, "You don't look so terrible yourself."

We walked over to the Chapel of the Bells, one of those neon marriage joints on the strip. The town was chiming all around us. The moon was low in the desert, where the mob dumps its bodies and the lizards dream of mice. I took her hand. She took my arm. We were grinning like mad. Before the vows, the chaplain said, "For an extra fifteen bucks, you can have organ music."

I said, "Yeah, just give us what you got and do it fast. The lady has a show."

We spent summers in Kennebunkport, Maine, and eventually bought a house of our own. It's gorgeous up there, but there was never much for me to do. I get bored. I was a fish out of water, a Bronx Jew trapped in the sticks. One afternoon, when I was young and the sun shone down on my every adventure, I went to the local Kennebunkport club to play tennis. I had never been to this club. The courts were empty. I went to the woman behind the desk, gave my name, and asked for a court. She said, "I'm sorry, Mr. Weintraub, we have no courts."

I was confused. "But the place is empty," I told her.

"Perhaps you should try a different club," she said.

The reality of the situation slowly dawned on me. It was like the scene in *Gentlemen's Agreement* when Gregory Peck tries to check into a hotel as Phil Greenberg. I am sorry, Mr. Greenberg. We have no rooms.

I am sorry Mr. Weintraub. We have no courts.

WHINE-traub!

If you a Jew, where your horns?

I would like to say I raised a ruckus, tore the place up, stood there saying no, no, no, as Gregory Peck did in the movie. But the fact is, I just dropped my head and went home. Sometimes, the polite "No" registers more powerfully than even the blow to the face. The blow to the face you know how to respond to: with a blow to the face! But the polite "No," how do you respond to that? I was pissed off, angry, humiliated. I told Jane. She was really upset. She said, "No, it can't be."

Later, without my knowing, Jane told the story to an old Kennebunkport friend. This was George H. W. Bush, before politics or any of that. He was a businessman, his father was a senator. He called me later that same day. He said, "Hi, I'm George Bush, I'm a friend of Jane's, and I heard you like to play tennis."

I said, "Yeah, I like to play tennis."

He said, "Well, do you want to play in the morning at the club with my dad and my brother and myself?"

I said, "They don't want me at the club. I went over today, and they told me no Jews allowed."

"That's ridiculous," said Bush. "You want to play tomorrow morning, you can play with us."

So I went there to play with George Bush, his father, Senator Bush, and his brother. As we were leaving, Senator Bush asked me if I would like to be a member of the tennis club.

I said, "Yeah, I'd love to be a member."

He said, "Fine, we'll make you a member. George," he said, "go in and tell them I'm proposing Jerry for membership. If there's any problem, let me know." I became a member of the tennis club. Then they did the same thing at the yacht club and the golf club. So that was the end of the Jewish thing.

That's how I met George Bush. I loved him from the first moment. He would become one of my best friends. He was very young at that time, not yet in politics, just a businessman making his way. But as soon as you spoke to him, you knew he was going the distance. We grew up together, in our way, pushed each other, advised and helped each other. People in Hollywood were sometimes suspicious of this relationship, and did not understand it. I was, and still am, said to be one of the few Republicans in Hollywood. It was a headline. But I am not a Republican. I am an Independent, liberal on social issues, conservative on fiscal matters. I just happen to have a good friend named George Bush. And, as I explained, nothing is more important than a relationship. It trumps politics, party, club. People are what matter. In short, I'm for the man, and I've never met a better one than George Bush.

I feel I really must stop here and explain just how important George Bush has been in my life. He opened the world to me, took me everywhere and showed me everything. I love the man as you love a father or a brother, and appreciate everything he has done for me, and does for me still, which, most of all, is the gift of his friendship. Had I not met George and Barbara, my life would have been totally different. He changed the scope of everything. I was put into a world I never could have experienced in a million years. To be a close friend of the president of the United States is an awesome, awesome position. You have to know how to handle it. You can't go to him with nonsense and silly things. I never did. I went to him with some very important things, and he helped because he felt they were right. But I didn't bother him on a day-to-day basis. And yet we had an open relationship where I could tell him when I thought he was right and when I thought he was wrong. Very few people have that access to the most powerful man in the world. I stayed in the White House a lot. I stayed in the Lincoln Bedroom and the Queen's Bedroom. It was inspiring, for a kid from the Bronx, to be befriended by the president, and for him to open this oyster for me and have me at state dinners, to have me there when Gorbachev came and other world leaders came, introducing me to them, and to be very close to his whole cabinet... to Jim Baker, secretary of state, to Nick Brady, secretary of the treasury, to Bob Mosbacher, secretary of commerce, to John Sununu, his chief of staff, etc., etc. Bush made sure I was in the center of his universe. He opened me up to a network of people around the world. Everybody knew we were close. Everybody knew that I was embraced by this man. He made it very public; he didn't hide it. And he was very supportive when I had troubles. He was a great friend.

One night, years ago, when Bush was a congressman, we went for a walk in Washington, D.C., after the Alfalfa dinner. We passed the White House, which was all lit up, and I said, "I think you're going to live in that house someday."

"Don't be silly," he said.

But I knew it. I could see it in the way the other politicians gathered around him at the dinner—he was a natural leader.

In 1980, on the night that he was elected vice president, Bush was at my house in Beverly Hills, in my living room. He brought about twenty-five of his advisors. They had just come off the campaign trail and were exhausted. The election was over, and they had flown to California to see Reagan. I showed a film. (In it, Walter Matthau played the chief of the CIA, which I thought was appropriate, as Bush had had that same job.) James Baker fell asleep on the couch. We drank champagne and celebrated. It was a great honor for me, but Bush didn't look at it that way. To him, it was just a night at a friend's house. Later, when he became president, he used to take me to state dinners, meetings, everything. He had me to lunch with Mikhail Gorbachev, just the three of us, me, the president, and the premier. I did not stay in a hotel when I went to Washington. I stayed in the White House. (What a thrill, sleeping in the Lincoln Bedroom, with the Gettysburg Address under glass!) He took me behind the scenes, showed me how the world is wired at its highest reaches. How did it happen that this beautifully educated, perfectly bred, white Anglo-Saxon Protestant from New England became so friendly with this mutt from the Bronx? It's a question I've often asked myself. I think it's because he trusts me, and knows that I trust him. I'm not going to be one way with him, another way with someone else. For better or worse, I am still the same kid who ran away from the Bronx. Life is strange—you travel so far, do so much, but the people you look for at the end are often the same people you looked for at the beginning.

Over the years, Bush and I have played a lot of tennis and golf. Our friendship started on that court in Maine, and tennis and golf have been a continuing theme. One day, when Bush was president, he decided we should play a determining match. "You pick a partner and I pick a partner," he said, "and we'll finally settle it." So who does Bush recruit? The pro from his country club! He's president of the United States, and this is the best he can do? What a gentleman! He wants to win, but doesn't want to destroy me. Who do I recruit? Rod Laver, who was then living somewhere in California. We played at Bush's house in Kennebunkport. Laver walks out. The president says, "Oh, my God. It's Rod Laver! The greatest tennis player ever! I am so excited to meet you!"

"Tell you what," Bush said to Laver. "You be my partner."

I said, "No, Mr. President. He will not be your partner. He is my partner. You have already chosen your partner. The pro from your club."

As we walked out on the court, Laver said to me, "Do you want to let him win?"

"No," I said, "I want to beat him."

"How bad?"

"Bad."

"Okay," said Laver, "here is what we are going to do…"

And he explained how he would control each point, setting the ball up a foot or so in front of my racket. I just had to slam it home.

We took a picture at the end of the match. It's the president, posed as if dead on the court, with me and Laver standing over him, grinning.

All the King's Men

I have always been a believer in relationships, in strength in numbers and flying in a pack, which is why, in 1963, I combined my business with the businesses of two friends to form Management Three. It was me, Bernie Brillstein, and Marty Kummer. I had some acts, the biggest being Jane. Bernie had some acts, the biggest being Jim Henson and the Muppets; Marty had some acts, the biggest being Jack Paar. Together, we figured we could take over the world. Bernie died in 2008, Marty before that. More than friends, these men were family. I loved them. If you work with people you love, which, of course, is not always possible, the hard times become an epic adventure. If Bernie was around, he would tell you about the office we rented at Fifty-fifth and Lexington Avenue. He would tell you about the hundreds of nights we spent out in the city, in the nightclubs and dives, the cocktail tables crowded with martinis. We searched every nook and cranny for talent. I had set myself up as the outside man, the public face of Management Three, who had to be kept in good suits and luxury, as our potential clients would judge the health of the company by my appearance. I bought myself a Rolls-Royce and hired a driver, though

I could not afford them. I figured it was all about appearance, perception, as the man who rides in style often rides away with the big contract.

Bernie went to Los Angeles to open a West Coast office. Then I went out. This is when I made the full-time move to LA. Within a few years, I moved into the house that I have called home ever since. LA was wildly exciting in those years. The last of the old moguls were still around, as were the stars of Hollywood's Golden Age. Jimmy Stewart, Cary Grant, John Wayne, Rita Hayworth, Gene Kelly—I would come to know them all. People think New Yorkers of my generation, their memories swollen with egg cream and stickball and whatever, long for those old neighborhoods, but that is not true. What we miss, if anything, are the people, the world when it was crowded with crucial players. As for the place, I have always believed the West Coast has it over the East Coast in every way. Going from New York to LA, with its palm trees and swimming pools and white houses and green hills and Santa Ana winds, was excellent in a way it is hard to express. It was like stepping from the orchestra pit of the theater on Fordham Road in the Bronx up onto the screen. Things started to cook as soon as I was settled in LA. There were meetings, deals, parties, signings, but all of this was really just the prologue before the great early triumph of my career—the success that would make everything else possible.

I was in bed, Jane at my side. I always sleep with a notepad on the table so I can write down ideas that come in the night. That night, I saw Madison Square Garden in a dream, fronted by a huge marquee on which big, beautiful, red letters, lit against a blue velvet sky, read: JERRY WEINTRAUB PRESENTS ELVIS PRESLEY. My eyes clicked open like a camera shutter. I rolled over, started writing.

"What now?" asks Jane.

"I'm going to promote Elvis Presley," I tell her. "I'm going to take him to Madison Square Garden."

"That's crazy," she says. "You don't even know Elvis Presley."

"Not yet," I say, close the book, roll over, and am asleep before she can answer.

The next morning, I dug up a number for Colonel Tom Parker, the onetime carnie who had managed Elvis for years, got him on the phone, and said, "Colonel Parker, this is Jerry Weintraub. I would like to take Elvis Presley on the road."

The Colonel had a sly, deliberate way of talking. He took his time. You just knew he was grinning, chomping a cigar, turning it slowly in his mouth. He said, "Who are you, son?"

"This is Jerry Weintraub," I told him. "I have a strategy in mind, a way to take Elvis on the road that will mean a lot of money."

He said, "Look here, boy, in the first place, Elvis is not going on the road"—at this point, the mid to late sixties, Elvis was doing movies, and had not been on tour for years—"and, in the second, if he were to go on tour, which he's not, it would not be you taking him. I've got guys lined up for that job, people we need to take care of."

End of conversation.

If there's one piece of advice I can give to young people, to kids trying to break out of Brooklyn and Kankakee, it's this: persist, push, hang on, keep going, never give up. When the man says no, pretend you can't hear him. Look confused, stammer, say, "Huh?" Persistence—it's a cliché, but it happens to work. The person who makes it is the person who keeps on going after everyone else has quit. This is more important than intelligence, pedigree, even connections. Be dogged! Keep hitting that door until you bust it down! I have accomplished almost nothing on the first or second or even the third try—the breakthrough usually comes late, when everyone else has left the field.

I called the Colonel again the next morning.

"What can I do for you, son?"

"Hello, Colonel, this is Jerry Weintraub. I want to take Elvis out on the road."

"You don't give up, do you, boy?"

"No, Colonel, not when I know I'm right."

I called every day for months and months. I did not flip him in the course of one of those calls, but I had planted my name so deep in his brain he would never forget it. Whenever he thought of taking Elvis on tour, he thought of Jerry Weintraub.

One morning, about a year after the dream, the Colonel called me at home.

"Do you still want to take my boy out on the road?"

"Yes, Colonel."

"Well, I'll be at the roulette table at the Hilton International Hotel in Vegas tomorrow at nine A.M. You meet me there with a check for a million dollars, and he's yours."

Great. Wonderful. Terrific. Fantastic. My dream is coming true. All I have to do is raise more money than I have ever seen in my life, and do it in twenty-four hours. Back then, a million dollars was real money. Rockefellers, Carnegies—those were the only people that had money like that. I started making calls, banging on doors, calling in favors, promising, begging—anything to get the cash. This was my shot. I did not want to blow it. I stayed up all night, getting turned down again and again, flying on coffee and adrenaline. "No," "Don't have it," "Are you crazy?" "Who do you think I am?" "A million dollars?

Ha, ha, ha!" "You've lost your mind," "I will get back to you when my oil well hits"—these are the kinds of responses I was getting. I was desperate, running out of time.

Finally, late that night, I got a call back from an old friend. He said there was a guy in Seattle named Lester Smith who owned radio stations, lots of radio stations, and was a tremendous Elvis fan—*this guy might give you the money just to be in business with Presley.* So I called the guy—his business manager was on an extension—and I made the pitch. They wanted to see proposals, papers, and so on. I didn't blame them. I would want to see these things, too, but there was no time. "I would like to," I told him, "but I have just a few hours to get a check and meet Colonel Parker in Vegas. So, at this point, it's yes or no. You're going to have to trust me on the rest."

As he was saying yes, I was getting my keys, pulling on my coat, heading out the door. I went to the airport and got a plane. I stared out the window at the desert. I took a cab to the hotel, checked into my room, called the Colonel. "I'm getting the money," I told him, "but I'm going to need a little more time."

"All right," he said. "You have till three P.M. But that's it. You know where to meet me."

I rushed over to the bank, one of those cash-and-carry places downtown. What a sight! The place had a gold crown over the door and it was all purple and it looked less like a bank than a whorehouse. I went to the woman at the front desk. "My name is Jerry Weintraub," I told her. "I'm waiting for a million dollar wire transfer. I'm going to need a cashier's check for the same amount." She looked at me like I was nutty, maybe a bank robber. I had long hair in those days, sideburns and boots, and I was telling this girl I planned to leave there with a million dollars. I sat in a big chair, looking through the windows as I waited for the money to come in. It was a strange afternoon, spent suspended between my life as it had been and my life as it was going to be. Elvis was the biggest star in the world. If I took him on the road, if I promoted him, nothing would be the same. I knew that. Finally, after I had been daydreaming for two hours—I was pushing against the new deadline—the president of the bank, a young guy, asked me to follow him into his office.

"Your cashier's check is being prepared, Mr. Weintraub."

"Right."

"It's made out to Elvis Presley...One million dollars."

"Great."

"That's a lot of money."

"Yes, it sure is."

"What do you plan to do with it?"

"I'm taking Elvis on tour," I said.

This guy's eyes lit up. He said, "Do you need an accountant?"

"I know how you feel," I told him, "and let me think about it, but right now, I need to get that check and get over there or I'm going to miss the Colonel and no one will be going anywhere."

"Of course," he said, giving me the check, this monstrous check. I looked at it and shivered, folded it into my breast pocket, ran out, and caught a cab to the Hilton. I spotted the Colonel as soon as I walked onto the casino floor. You could not miss him. He was wearing a white cowboy hat and a ratty short-sleeved shirt, chomping a cigar. He looked like the guy ripping you off at the county fair. He was the hero of his own movie.

"Colonel Tom Parker?"

"You Jerry Weintraub?"

"Yes, sir."

He looked at me skeptically, through one eye, then asked, "You got the money?"

"I do."

"Wait a minute," he told me, "I want to finish this spin"—he was playing roulette, which is a sucker's game—then said, "Okay, follow me."

We went up to his suite, where he had a little office. He sat behind his desk, then said, "Let's have it."

I took the check out of my pocket, unfolded it, handed it to him. He looked at it for a moment, unlocked a safe, put the check inside, then said, "Okay, Jerry, what do you want to do with my boy?"

"Take him out on the road."

"Good! Let's do it."

Thinking back, I realize there were no papers, no contracts, no nothing. I handed him the check, he took the check, that's it.

The Colonel was amazing. As an old carnie, he really understood how to package and sell. He began in the music business in the 1940s promoting country acts like Minnie Pearl and Hank Snow and Eddie Arnold, but he did not get into the chips until he signed Elvis to a management contract in 1954. He built Presley's career from there, moving him from Sun Records to RCA Victor, getting him into movies, and, in the process, turning the kid from Tupelo into the king of rock and roll. Some critics thought Elvis lost authenticity in the process, but the Colonel was always a big marketing man. If you were walking this earth, he wanted to sell to you. He was, in this way, a true egalitarian. He wanted no one left out. He once scolded me, saying, "To you guys from the coasts, the country is New York and LA. Everything in between is just the blur you fly over. But

I'll tell you, that blur is where the audience lives and where you make your money."

I remember the first time I went to his house. He had a statue garden in the yard, with these odd ceramic animals and plastic flamingos. His taste was not my taste—it came from the carnival, the midway. To him, art was a pink elephant. But he taught me how to look at other parts of America. To understand this country, you must understand the paintings in the Whitney Museum in New York, or know how to pretend to, but you must also understand the flamingos in Colonel Tom's garden. To this day, if you go to my office at Warner Bros., you will see, out front, two plastic flamingos in the grass. This is to remind me where I come from: from the Bronx, yes, but also from the school of Colonel Tom Parker, who taught me how to hawk my wares in every part of America.

People later said the Colonel stole from Elvis, took too much, or did not treat him right. He was vilified. But, as far as I'm concerned, none of that's true. The Colonel never stole anything from Elvis. If he had, I would have known it. I was there. Elvis made all the artistic decisions and did exactly what he wanted to do. Business and promotion—that was what the Colonel cared about. As for the movies, which some people didn't like, Colonel Parker had just two rules. One: It had to have ten songs, because ten songs made a record. Two: Elvis got paid one million dollars. This neat sum, one million, the Colonel loved it. It rolled off his tongue.

Years later, I was at a meeting at the Beverly Wilshire with Colonel Parker and Hal Wallis, a Paramount producer who worked with Elvis on many movies, including *Love Me Tender*. He wanted Elvis for *Harum Scarum*, a Rudolph Valentino–type film. After going through various details, the men finally got to the salary. "Well, look, Colonel, I know the usual terms," said

Wallis, "but this is a different kind of movie, with a different kind of budget. We can't pay Elvis a million dollars."

"You know what he gets," said the Colonel. "Give us the money, tell us where to be, and we'll make a movie. If not, I'm not sure why you're here."

"You don't understand," said Wallis. "This is an Academy Award film. Elvis is going to win the Academy Award."

"Oh, you're right, I didn't understand," said the Colonel. "An Academy Award! That *is* something. Tell you what, Hal. You give me a million dollars, and when he gets the Academy Award, I will give you back five hundred thousand."

Wallis then went directly to Elvis. "I have something amazing for you," he said. "You will play a role like Rudolph Valentino would have played. You will look like Valentino in *The Sheik*. He was the most handsome man in the world; you will be more handsome. This is going to make you into a great actor as well as a movie star."

"Okay," said Elvis, "but who was Valentino? I don't know anything about him."

"We'll get you books," says Wallis. "You'll learn all about him."

So Elvis starts reading up on Valentino, and learns, among other things, that Valentino was nasty, temperamental, and hard to work with, and always came late to the set. So what does Elvis do? Well, he's an actor now. He becomes Valentino. He behaves in a way he never behaved. If you wanted to do a picture with Elvis in eighteen days, it was done in eighteen days. If you wanted him on the set at 6:00 A.M., he was there at 5:30. Now he's coming late and he is leaving early, disappearing, ignoring direction. Nobody can control him. Hal Wallis finally calls the Colonel. He says, "Colonel, you've got to do something about Elvis."

The Colonel says, "It's very simple, Hal. Tell him he's not Rudolph Valentino."

That, as far as I know, was the extent of the Colonel's creative involvement in Presley's career.

After I gave the Colonel the cashier's check, he brought me to meet Elvis, who had a suite in the Hilton International. He must've been performing there at the time.

We knocked on the door, went in, and there was Elvis. He was in his thirties, about five years older than I was. It was his Sun God phase, scarves, flare-legged jumpsuits, white boots, hair long and breaking like a wave from forehead to the nape of his neck. Hal Wallis was right. He was a handsome man. "This is Jerry Weintraub," the Colonel told him. "He's the man I told you about, who paid a million dollars for you. He's going to work with us."

Elvis shook my hand and said, "It's an honor, sir. I appreciate it. There is only one thing I ask when we're on the road: Please make sure, when I perform, that every seat is filled. And please make sure my fans are in the front rows—not the big shots."

Elvis was older than me. He was also the biggest star in the world. Yet he called me sir. It's how he was raised. He was uneducated and country, but really, in many ways, a true gentleman. What happened to him later, with the drugs and the weight, was a tragedy.

We went on the road a few weeks after that. We picked the cities and dates and arenas. I did all this with Tom Hulett, who was my partner in the concert business. We did everything together. It was a groundbreaking tour. It changed the nature of the business. Before that, the concert business had been broken into territories, each region of the country controlled by a local promoter—who picked the venue, sold the tickets, arranged the publicity, and so on. There was no such thing as a national tour. An artist moved from fiefdom to fiefdom, and the manager cut deals with local power brokers—the man who "owned" Philadelphia, the man who "owned" Buffalo—who made subsidiary deals with local police, local unions, local arena operators. This system was byzantine and wasteful. At each step, the local promoter paid off and kicked back, cut sweetheart deals, cooked the books, even took profits from the hit tours to pay for the dogs. When the artists came off the road, they always had less money than they believed they had earned.

But if you tried to go around the local promoters and cut your own deals, you would find yourself frozen out of the territory. No one would rent you the hall if it was not through the local guy, who was, after all, kicking money back to the operator. But the balance changed when I was booking Elvis. I was finally able to cut deals directly with the arenas, as no one would turn away the show. Elvis was simply too big. If you said no, someone else would say yes, meaning you would miss out on the biggest payday ever. This was what I had meant when I told the Colonel I had a better way to take Elvis on the road. I cut out the middleman, which drove down costs and increased profits, meaning more money for everyone. What's more, I structured the deal as a production, like a play, in which Elvis, the Colonel, and I split the profits. I was not an agent taking a percentage, I was a partner taking a share. If Elvis saved money, I saved money; if Elvis was enriched, I was enriched. Since one person booked the entire tour, there were also economies of scale. I got better deals because I put on more shows. As a result, artists who signed with me—I am talking about later, after I went out with Elvis—made more money.

Which attracted more artists. Which meant the local operators, if they wanted shows for their arenas, had to work with me. This is how I broke the old system.

None of this was easy. Every local promoter wanted me destroyed. I was ending their reign. It was a tremendous fight, but I knew if I came out intact I would have a new livelihood: This became my company, Concerts West, which, within a few years, was the largest concert business in the world. In this way, I became the most hated man in the industry. But as Don Corleone said, "It's better to be feared than loved."

When I booked that first Elvis tour, I did not know what I was doing. I was such a neophyte. Being as naïve as I was about the business, I had Elvis open on the Fourth of July in Miami Beach. Have you ever been to Miami Beach in the middle of July? It's a swamp. It's five million degrees and humid as hell. No one is there, and no one should be. We booked the convention center, which had ten thousand seats.

About two weeks out, I called the guy who ran the box office. I asked him how we were doing.

"Great," he said. "We're sold out."

"Really? Sold out? Already? That's fantastic."

I thought for a moment, then said, "Hey, what do you think of a matinee?"

"Great!" he said. "You'll have no problem selling it. Demand is through the roof."

I went back and asked the Colonel.

"Yeah, yeah," he said. "Book it."

One day. Two shows. Twenty thousand seats. Big-time show business.

As soon as we stepped off the plane in Miami, we needed a shower. The heat waves shimmered. Anything more than fifty yards away looked like a mirage. The concierge from the Fontainebleau sent a limousine to pick us up. I got in, smiling. The Colonel just stood there.

"Hey, come on," I said. "What are you waiting for?"

He said, "Sorry, son, but that just ain't my kind of fancy."

Instead, he climbed into the station wagon that had been sent for the luggage.

I dropped off my bags and went to the arena.

I walked into the box office and asked for the guy I had been talking to on the phone. I wanted to check the gate. The concert was the next afternoon. He was sitting in the office, holding this huge stack of tickets, smiling.

"What are those?" I asked.

"What are what, Mr. Weintraub?"

"In your hand," I said.

"These are your tickets," he said. "For Elvis. The matinee."

"Are people coming to pick them up?" I asked.

"No, Mr. Weintraub. These are the tickets that have not sold."

"What do you mean? You said you would sell them all."

There were maybe five thousand tickets in his hand—half the house. My mind was racing, a single word tolling in my mind: disaster, disaster, disaster! What did Elvis tell me, his one thing? "I just don't want to sing to any empty seats."

I got close to the ticket seller, looked into his cold, pinprick eyes. "Why did you tell me we were sold out?" I asked.

He shrugged and said, "I was just telling you what you wanted to hear."

I went wild, grabbed him by the shirt, shook him, swearing. He grinned. I picked him up, slammed him into the wall. People came running. They pulled me off. Someone said, "Take it easy. You're gonna kill him!" I stormed out, trying to cool down, trying to think. *My career is going to be over before it begins.* I walked outside, then followed the street to the beach. I was thinking about the concert, about what would happen when Elvis saw all those empty seats. *What can I do? Give away the tickets, confess to Elvis, throw myself on the mercy of the Colonel?*

On the way back to the arena, I passed the county jail, a windowless fortress just across from the Civic Center. I wandered around the arena until Elvis showed up with his entourage for rehearsal and sound check. I pulled the Colonel aside.

"What's happening, son?" he asked.

"Well, Colonel, we have a problem," I told him.

"Oh, we do," he said. "What's our problem?"

"It seems I was misled before I booked the matinee," I said, "and now I'm stuck with five thousand unsold seats."

He pushed his hat back and said, "Well, son, as far as I can tell, we don't have a problem. You have a problem."

"Yeah, well, what should I do?" I asked.

"I'll tell you what you should do," he said. "You should fix your problem."

He went back to his entourage, and I went back to the hotel. I got in bed. I tossed and turned. When I finally fell sleep, I had nightmares, a tiny Elvis, with his cape and flare boots, kung fu kicking before an empty house, storming offstage, shouting, WHINE-traub! WHINE-traub!

I woke up early and went to the arena. I stood in the aisles and studied the seats. I noticed that bolts secured each of the seats to the floor. Meaning these could be unscrewed and carried away. *How long would it take to unscrew five thousand seats, how many men would it take?* I wandered over to the jailhouse

I had seen the day before, asked for the person in charge, and soon found myself talking to the sheriff. I don't remember what he looked like, so imagine him as you want—a trim, officious, bureaucrat, or a big, burly southern lawman, the sort played by Jackie Gleason in *Cannonball Run*. I moved a pile of money from my pocket to his pocket.

"What can I do for you?" he asked.

"I want to take five thousand seats out of the convention center, hide them for a few hours, then, before the nighttime show, put them right back in," I said. "Can you help me?"

"No problem."

A few hours later, the sheriff showed up with dozens of prisoners, men in orange jumpsuits who unscrewed and carried away the seats, which they piled in the parking lot and covered with a blue tarp. In my mind, I still see that blue tarp hiding the unsold seats. It is one of several images that, spliced together, tell the story of my career. The jewelry bag with my initials is the life I did not live. The seats rising from second base to the grandstand is the audience that must be attracted, satisfied, sold. The blue tarp is the need to innovate and improvise.

Elvis sang the matinee. It was great. Not an empty seat in the house. Then, as he rested between shows, the prisoners went back to work, tearing away the tarp, carrying the seats back to the arena, screwing them into the floor. The second show was even better. Elvis sang all his hits. Between songs, he dabbed sweat from his face with a scarf, then tossed the scarf to the women near the stage, who fought over it, smelled it, passed out. I went back to the Fontainebleau hotel with Elvis. He was spent, exhilarated but depleted, having given everything away. "You know, Jerry, it's amazing," he told me. "The crowd was good in the afternoon, but it's always so much better at night."

We were on the road for just under a month. I was working as a kind of advance man, traveling a day or two ahead of the tour, checking into hotels, meeting security, scouting arenas. I was learning the ups and downs and constant crises of life on the road. Now and then, I pursued a whim or a moneymaking scheme of my own. There was, for example, the near disaster of the scarves (this happened on a later tour). Having seen the girls fight over the scarves Elvis tossed from the stage—you could see the flurry, the snap of teeth—I decided to order the kind of scarves used by Elvis and sell them at the concession stands. Turn a nice little profit. The first boxes reached me at the Pontiac Dome in Detroit, Michigan. Seventy-five thousand seats, sold out, New Year's Eve. I had ordered thirty-five thousand scarves, ten cents apiece, made in Hong Kong, with Elvis's picture on them. I remember walking past the concession as the fans came in from the parking lot. They stood in line to buy T-shirts, mugs, key chains, but no one seemed interested in my scarves. During intermission, the head of concessions came up to me, shaking his head. "I'm so sorry, Mr. Weintraub, but we're not selling the scarves," he said. "It's just not going to work."

I walked into the dressing room, moping, depressed. Elvis saw me sitting in a chair with my head down. "What's wrong?" he asked. "You look terrible."

"I have a problem."

"What?"

I told him about the scarves.

"If I fix it," he said, "will you smile?"

"How are you going to fix it?"

"Don't worry," he said. "Just tell me: Will you smile?"

"Of course," I said. "I'm starting to smile just thinking about it."

So what does he do? He goes out onstage, does a number, gets the crowd going wild, stops, puts his hand on his forehead, salutelike, as if trying to make out something far away, then says, "You know, I can't see anything or anyone from up here. Turn on the lights."

The lights come up, he blinks, eyes asquint.

"I still can't see," he says. "Tell you what. I'm going to take a five-minute break. Go out to the concession. They have scarves. I want everyone to get a scarf and wave it so I can see where you are."

In those five minutes, the concessionaires sold every scarf in the arena. Then, as Elvis was walking back on stage, he looked at me and said, "Are you smiling now?"

That first tour ended in San Diego. I was standing backstage on the last night, looking through the curtain at the crowd, dazed, shell-shocked. Just then, amid all this drifting and dreaming—I was wearing my crocodile boots—the Colonel whacked me on the shoulder with his cane. "Come with me," he said. "We need to talk."

He had a big guy following him with two huge suitcases. We went through the tunnels to a little door, an electrical closet. There was a table inside, a lightbulb, and a bunch of machinery. The Colonel told the big guy where to put the bags, then said, "Beat it. I need to talk to Jerry alone."

The Colonel locked the door. "Get the bags up on the table," he told me. "Open them."

It was like a scene in an old pirate movie, in which the swashbuckler looks into the treasure chest and the glow of doubloons reflects off his face. These cases were filled with money, tens, twenties, fifties, all cash. As if we had robbed a bank. "Pour it on the table," said the Colonel.

"What's this?" I asked.

"The money from the concessions," he said. "T-shirts and collectibles. Half of it's yours."

"No, I had nothing to do with that," I said. "Just the tickets. Just the shows."

The Colonel was already giving me an incredibly generous deal: an even split. I got half, and the Colonel and Elvis together got half.

"When I have a partner," he told me. "I have a partner. Now pile up that money."

It was a mountain of bills, some stained with ketchup, some stained with chives, stacked on the table. The Colonel said, "Stand back," then raised his cane and brought it down hard on the pile, dividing it into two huge piles, which he pushed apart with the cane, saying, "That side yours, this side mine . . . Is that fair?"

"Sure," I said. "It's more than fair."

The tour lasted just six weeks, but it changed everything. Like what happens when you put your picture in a Xerox and press enlarge, enlarge, enlarge. I went on tour at twenty-six as just another young talent manager, but when I came back, I was a millionaire.

The Colonel had houses in LA and Palm Springs. I was with him constantly, in every kind of mood and weather, when he was happy and money was coming in, and when he was ailing and old. No matter how rich he became, he was always ready for a new idea. He was, after all, a carnival man. Take, for example, the Gordon Mills affair, maybe my greatest moneymaking idea that did not come off.

The phone rings in the middle of the night. It's Elvis. He is angry and paranoid, pacing the halls of Graceland.

"Is that Jerry?" he asks.

"Yeah, Elvis. It's me. What's up?"

"I don't know what I'm doing here," he says. "I just don't know."

"What's wrong, Elvis?"

"The Colonel," he says. "I don't need him. I'm done with the Colonel."

"Come on, Elvis."

"Listen, Jerry, you should be my manager."

This is not unusual, these freaked-out, middle-of-the-night calls made by talent—decisions made, then unmade in the morning. Especially when the artist is as brilliant and isolated as Elvis. The Beatles had each other, and Sinatra, well, Sinatra was from another era, but Elvis, who was bigger than all of them, was alone.

I said, "Look, Elvis. I am sorry, but I can't. That's not going to happen."

We talked for a little, then hung up. I could not fall back asleep. I stared at the ceiling, thinking. A few days before, I had seen a copy of *Life* magazine with a man named Gordon Mills on the cover, a music manager from London. According to the article, his management company, MAM, which was traded on the London Stock Exchange, was the most successful in the industry, representing two of the three biggest stars in the world: Tom Jones and Engelbert Humperdinck. Now it happened that these stars were numbers two and three. Elvis was number one.

I went to see the Colonel at six the next morning. He was drinking coffee. I threw *Life* magazine in front of him.

"What's this?" he asked.

"That," I said, "is Gordon Mills."

"Yeah, so?"

"Look, Colonel, what if I told you I had a way to make a hundred million bucks just like that?"

"I would tell you to keep talking," he said.

"I'm not going to bullshit you," I told him. "Elvis called me in the middle of the night and said he wants to get rid of you and make me his manager."

The Colonel made a noise like this: "Ahhhieeee."

I said, "Now, Colonel, I've had enough clients, done enough business, and been around long enough to know it doesn't mean anything. Elvis is *you and Elvis*. I get that. But it gave me an idea, seeing as he's talking about getting a new manager, and this is where the hundred million bucks comes in."

"Go on."

"This guy, Gordon Mills, has a publicly traded management company. He also has two of the three biggest recording artists in the world. Now here's my idea: We sell him Elvis's management contract. In name only. It will still be you running the show, but this guy will hold the paper. We structure this deal in stock, so Mills gets the contract and we—me, you, Elvis—get shares in his company. Lots of shares. Then, when word gets out that Gordon Mills has Tom Jones, Engelbert Humperdinck, *and* Elvis Presley, well, the share price goes through the roof. And we clear a hundred million easy."

"Yeah," said the Colonel. "Do it."

I called Gordon Mills and told him I had an idea, a surefire moneymaker.

"Great," he said. "Come over and explain it."

I would never sell an idea like this on the phone. It's still that way. I need to sit with a person, to watch him, read his eyes and hands, see if he is just as excited as I am, if I'm coming across.

I got on a plane and flew over. Gordon Mills lived in a mansion outside London. He had his own zoo. (A lot of rich people in England have zoos.) He was a poor kid from the East End who had made it all the way to a private zoo. We talked in his garden. Giraffes wandered by, zebras, and tigers. A lion cub pissed my lap! I explained the plan: how we would sell Elvis but not sell Elvis, how he would give us shares, how the stock price would rise. Gordon nodded through this, thinking Elvis, Elvis, then said, "Fantastic, Jerry! Let's do it!"

"Now look, Gordon, I want to make sure you understand the situation," I said. "You are not really going to manage Elvis. He won't accept that. I am talking about a business arrangement. You will sign the contracts and get commissions, but on the ground we will continue as we have been: I will handle the concerts, the Colonel will handle everything else; you will be his manager in name only. You will not talk to Elvis, or try to shape his career, and you will have absolutely no creative input. Get it?"

"Yes, yes, great. Let's do it."

"That's the first caveat," I said. "Here's the second: You can't tell anybody about this. I don't want to pick up the *Daily Telegraph* or the *Sun* and see splattered all over the pages, 'Gordon Mills to Be Elvis's Manager.' You can have that later, but not now. You've got to wait for that."

"Great, let's do it."

A few weeks later, Gordon Mills came to Vegas. The Colonel was there, too. It took me two weeks to set up a meeting. Tom Jones worked at Caesars and Elvis worked at the Hilton.

Each manager wanted to meet on his home turf. I shuttled back and forth like Kissinger. I finally fixed a date at the Hilton. The Colonel won that round. He showed up in cowboy suit and hat. He sat on one side of the table, and Gordon sat on the other. These men had egos bigger than the moon. They would not talk to each other. Everything had to go through me. The Colonel would say, "Tell him he's not to travel with us." Gordon would say, "Tell him Elvis must make himself amenable to European dates." It went back and forth like that for hours, but I finally got the parameters fixed. Then, just as we were leaving, Gordon said, "Hey, Jerry, as long as I'm here, I would love to see Elvis perform."

"No problem," I said. "I'll get you seats."

"There will be eighteen of us," he said.

"What do you mean, eighteen of you?" I asked. "Who's eighteen?"

"Well, you know, my arranger, my public relations people, my this, my that…"

I said, "Look, Gordon, I was very clear about this. No creative input. You'll blow the whole deal."

"No, I understand," he said. "They just want to see Elvis."
Okay.

After the show, Gordon came backstage. We were talking. He said, "You know, Jerry, I would love to meet Elvis. Just say hello."

"Okay, I'll bring you over."

Elvis walked out of his dressing room, smiling, exhilarated.

I said, "Elvis, this is Gordon Mills. The man I told you about, that situation we're going to do."

I had explained the plan to Elvis. He was fine with it, one, because it would mean a lot of money, and two, because nothing would change.

Elvis said, "Oh, yes, Mr. Mills, it's a great pleasure to meet you, sir. Jerry told me all about this, it sounds like a terrific thing. Very excited about it."

Then Gordon said—and here's the kicker; it still kills me, all these years later—"You know, Elvis, I wanted to talk to you about the capes you wear in the show. I have some ideas."

They talked for a minute, Gordon gesticulating, Elvis, head down, like a boxer in the corner, nodding, "Yes, sir," "Yes, sir," "Yes, sir."

Elvis then said, "Can you excuse me, Mr. Mills?" and went into his dressing room.

Gordon turned to me, smiling, and said, "Oh, that went well! What a charming man!"

A second later, one of Elvis's guys came over and whispered in my ear: "Jerry, Elvis wants to see you right away."

That was the end of Gordon Mills.

There's something to be learned from this story. It shows how, even if you have the greatest script in the world, it won't work if the actors don't play their parts.

The Colonel and I were like father and son. We loved each other, but fought all the time. He used to get up early on the road, five, five-thirty in the morning, then go down to the free buffet. He would smoke his cigar and eat bacon and eggs surrounded by the lackeys who hung on his every word. I usually sat with them, but one morning—this was later—I woke up cranky and decided to eat alone. I got my food, walked by the Colonel's table, sat by myself in the corner.

He called over, "What are you, some kind of a big shot?"

I ignored him.

He said, "Hey, can't you hear me, big shot?"

I said, "What, am I bothering you?"

You were never supposed to challenge the Colonel in front of his people. He believed it undermined his authority.

He shouted, "What's wrong with you?"

"I'm eating my breakfast," I told him. "I want to be alone."

"Oh, you want to be alone?" he said. "Good. Be alone. You're fired!"

"I'm fired? No problem. You owe me a million dollars for this tour so far. Let me have my million bucks, and I'm gone."

Of course, I did not want to get fired, but I knew he would never give me a million dollars.

He stormed over to my table. "All right, big shot, follow me."

He acted like he was taking me to his room for the payout. We got up there, a stuffy motel suite, bed unmade, clothes everywhere. He walked to the bureau, opened the swinging doors and there, inside, he had made up a shrine to the Buddha. There were candles and incense set around a gold sculpture of Buddha, with his belly and grinning face and grand fleshy ears. The Colonel started lighting the candles.

"What the hell is happening?" I asked.

"We have to ask the Buddha what to do," he said.

He rubbed the Buddha's belly. He was such a con man. He said, "Tell me, O great Buddha, do you think we should keep Jerry Weintraub? Or should we let him go?"

He closed his eyes, as if he were meditating, communicating with the sages, then said to me, "The Buddha hasn't made up his mind yet."

The Colonel mumbled something, leaned in as if he was listening, then said, "It's the opinion of the Buddha that if you apologize in front of the boys all will be forgotten and it will be as it was before."

"I'm not apologizing," I said. "Tell that to the Buddha."

"You're not apologizing?"

"That's right. Tell the Buddha."

The Colonel closed his eyes, mumbled, nodded.

"The Buddha is very angry," he told me. "The Buddha says, 'Take Jerry Weintraub to the airport.'"

He blew out the candles and closed the cabinet. We went down to the van. The boys rode along. We got on the highway. I had my luggage and everything. We drove through town, past the arena. The Colonel was watching me, waiting for me to buckle. I did not buckle. I stared straight ahead. We saw the first signs for the airport. "All right, all right," he said. "Pull over."

The van stopped; the Colonel jumped out.

"Come on," he told me. "We need to talk."

He said, "Look, Jerry. You have to apologize. You have to say you were wrong. In front of everybody. All these boys work for me, and what you are doing can destroy everything."

"But I wasn't wrong," I told him. "I just wanted to have my breakfast alone."

"It's important to me that you apologize," he said. "Do it for me and later on I will do something for you."

"Fine," I told him. "What do you want me to say?"

"I want you to say that you are sorry, that you made a mistake, and that you shouldn't have done what you did."

"But I didn't do anything."

"It doesn't matter. Just say it."

We got back into the van and went to the arena. When we got out, with all the boys standing around, the Colonel said, "Jerry has something he would like to say."

"I am sorry," I told them, "I made a mistake, I should not have done what I did, and I will never do it again."

But I used that promise, the Colonel's price—"Do it for me and later on I will do something for you"—many times over the years. There is a lesson in this: Let the other guy save face with his people, but keep score.

Years later, the Colonel was living in Las Vegas, working as an advisor to Hilton Hotels. He was a great man, and still he died like most men die, little by little, then all at once. He had a stroke on January 21, 1997. He was eighty-seven years old. I was a pallbearer at his funeral and gave a eulogy, paying my respects to one of the last great showmen, and, more important, to a mentor and a true friend.

Old Blue Eyes

Working with Elvis made me rich, taught me show business, made me a player. I did not have to hustle quite as much. Once you've established yourself, you can, to some extent, let business find you. You become a beacon, a door into a better life. "Can you do for me what you did for Elvis?" In other words, people seek you out.

One afternoon, as I was reading through contracts, or whatever—I mean, who can remember?—the telephone rang.

"Hello."

"Is this Jerry Weintraub?"

"Yes."

The voice on the other end touched a sweet spot in the back of my brain. I knew it, but was not sure from where.

"Jerry, you and I need to talk business."

"Who is this?"

"Frank Sinatra."

"Oh, come on," I said. "Who is it really?"

"This is Frank Sinatra, Jerry, but I want you to call me Francis."

Now, you have to understand, for me, yes, there was Perry

Como, and the Beatles, and the Four Seasons, and Elvis, but Sinatra was it. Head and shoulders above the rest. He was my idol, who I went to see when I was not working, when I was low down and in need of a pick-me-up, and when I was flying high and wanted to celebrate. I was in love with this man, or the man he was in his music, before I ever shook his hand. More than just a performer, he was a symbol. He was Vegas and the high life, the epitome of cool, but also one of us, a kid from Hoboken, who struggled on the same streets and dreamed the same dreams. He had been challenged but persisted. He was tough, too, and did not let himself get pushed around. He was Maggio in *From Here to Eternity*, for godsakes! In short, he was you as you dreamed you might be. By the early seventies, when I knew him, he was beyond the recklessness of youth, the ups and downs, Ava Gardner, the feud with Warner Bros. He was in the highest realm of show business. He was royalty. Then there was his music, how he wrapped himself up in each song and turned everything into an anthem. His records became the soundtrack of your life. To this day, if you look in my car, you will find only Sinatra CDs. Which is why, when the call came like that, out of the blue, I wondered if I was being hoaxed.

"Yes, Mr. Sinatra."

"Please, call me Francis."

"Okay, Francis. How can I help you?"

"I want to meet."

"Great. When?"

"Look, kid, when I say I want to meet, that means now."

"Where?"

"Go to the Santa Monica airport. My plane is waiting. It will bring you to Palm Springs."

"I would love to, Mr. Sinatra. But it's the middle of the day. I have meetings."

"Call me Francis."

"Okay, Francis."

"Now, do what I say. Go to the airport. You will be home in time for dinner."

"Yes, Francis."

I drove to Santa Monica, got on the plane.

A driver picked me up on the runway in Palm Springs. We drove through hills studded with wood and glass houses, each turned, like a flower, toward the sun. Sinatra met me at his front door, shook my hand, brought me in. He was slender and handsome, always with a half smile, always fixing a drink, his words commented on by his famously blue eyes, which, unless he was angry or depressed, and he got very depressed, seemed to be saying, "Can you believe our lives? Can you believe how much fun we're having?" Let's say he was wearing chinos, white loafers, silk socks, and a V-neck sweater—the man could dress. We talked. This was 1972. Frank had "retired" the year before. It was one of the many retirements he announced then unannounced. He went in and out of the ring more times than Muhammad Ali. The real champions are torn: They want to go out on top, leaving an image of their best selves lingering before the public, but cannot stand to stay out of the fight.

Frank tapped my knee. "Look, Jerry," he said, "I've seen what you've done with Elvis. Very impressive. I'm thinking of coming out of retirement. Do you think I can play those same kind of rooms?"

"I don't see why not."

Of course, I would not put Sinatra in the exact same rooms

where Elvis was singing. These were different performers. Elvis was for the masses, for the people in the little towns between the big towns, the great crowds that filled the fields of the state fair. Sinatra was for the Italians and Jews, for the city people. He was urban. But the point remained—I could put Frank into new joints, bigger joints, the sort of arenas where crooners had never performed.

"Well, Okay," said Sinatra, "let's say that happened: Where would you start me?"

"Frank Sinatra? Well. Frank Sinatra has to open at Carnegie Hall."

I said this quickly, decisively, as if there was no other answer; a sense of certainty is what management is selling.

"Well, yes," said Sinatra. "Carnegie Hall sounds interesting."

He stood up, walked around the room, shaking the ice in his glass. "Okay, good," he said, "let's go with this."

"Go with what?"

"I want you to book a tour," said Sinatra. "I want you to handle this tour as I come out of retirement."

I got quiet, looked out the windows.

"What is it, kid?" asked Sinatra.

I said, "Look, Mr. Sinatra, I don't want you to take this the wrong way..."

"Francis, please. My name is Francis Albert Sinatra."

"Okay, Francis, I don't want you to take this the wrong way, but I have heard, just being around, talking to people, that sometimes, now and then, and again, don't take this the wrong way, you don't show up—you make the date, but don't turn up for the show."

He put down his drink, turned, and looked at me—his eyes were not humorous anymore, but icy blue. We didn't know each other, and, looking back, I suppose I was accusing him of being unprofessional. He said, "Are you crazy, coming into my house, talking to me like that? What's wrong with you?"

I said, "Look, no disrespect, Francis, but that's what I heard. And my career is just getting started. And I'm doing great. I'm a millionaire already. And I don't want to get into something I can't handle."

And he pointed his finger at me, and I'll never forget this, and said, "Here's what we're going to do. You and I, the two of us here, we're going to shake hands. And we're going to promise. I'm never going to disappoint you. And you know what, kid? You're never going to disappoint me, are you?"

I said, "No, Francis, I will never disappoint you."

And we shook hands, had another drink, and that was it. Once Frank Sinatra, excuse me, Francis, made a decision, it stayed made. He was loyal, a great man. Being accepted by Sinatra, entering his circle, that fraternity of knock-around guys, Dino, Jilly, Sammy, was one of the honors of my life. It was also one of the best possible credentials. It was Old Blue Eyes telling the guy at the desk, "Take care of him—he's one of mine."

We opened at Carnegie Hall. I had ditched my cowboy hat and jeans for a tux. I had slipped out of Elvis Country into Sinatra Land. This is another part of the job: being able to cross frontiers, move from culture to culture, making everyone believe you are a fully committed citizen of each. The curtain was called for 8:00 P.M. This was a black tie deal. Celebrities up the wazoo. Everyone was there. I'm not going to give you a list, but close your eyes and think of who was big in the 1970s: Well, they were there. I was backstage at 7:59. The house was empty. The people were in the street or in the lobby, fashionably late. You call the show for 8:00, they arrive at 8:35. New York. I'm staring through the curtain, wondering what kind of delay we're looking at, when there's a tap on my shoulder. It's Frank—excuse me, Francis—in his tux, dapper as hell.

"Jerry," he said, "it's eight P.M. Let's go."

"Yeah, but, Frank, the house is empty—no one is sitting down."

"Believe me," he said, "it will be like magic: When I start singing, they will be in their seats."

He turned, walked on stage, hit the first note, and BAM, the house was full.

On that first tour, I learned something new almost every night. Watching Sinatra work an audience of twenty thousand, take them up, bring them down, leave them in a kind of ecstatic high helped me in the movie business later on. It taught me how to structure a story: act one, act two, act three. Where did I go to school? Not to Harvard, Princeton, Stanford. I went to the school of Sinatra. I sat in his class every night. And while I was sitting there learning, I was making millions of dollars.

But the best part of working with Sinatra was not the tours, or the concerts, or even the money. It was the friendship, the camaraderie, the sense of being in it with the boys, the Chairman and the rest of the Rat Pack. When Frank was in LA, we were at Chasen's three nights a week, lighting it up, drinking and laughing. It was always a party. You knew where it started, but not where it would end. One night, we met at Chasen's and the next thing I know we're at a poker table at Frank's house in Palm Springs, playing big stakes. The game went on and on. At some point, George Hamilton came in. He was a friend of mine. He said, "Jerry, the house across from me is being sold in foreclosure. Thirty thousand. You should buy it. You won't have to rent anymore. But you have to buy it today."

"George, can't you see I'm in the middle of a game?"

"Yeah, sure, but it's a hell of a deal."

"You've seen this house?"

"Yeah, it's a beauty."

"Okay, if it's so great, buy it."

I write a check for thirty thousand, at least that's what they told me, because I forgot all about it a minute after it happened.

A few months later, Jane went to the desert to look at houses. We rented every winter. She found something she liked, then called our accountant to get money for the deposit.

"Why are you renting?" he asked her. "Jerry owns a house in Palm Springs."

She called me in a rage: "What the hell is going on? The accountant tells me you own a house in Palm Springs. How dare you! You have a girl set up down there? How dare you do this to me!"

I said, "What? No, no. That's crazy, absolute bullshit, not true. I own nothing in the desert."

I called the accountant. "What is this craziness?" I asked him. "You're telling Jane I own a house in Palm Springs? What's wrong with you?"

"But you do, Jerry."

"Do what?"

"You do own a house in Palm Springs."

"I do not. You're out of your mind."

"Jerry, you do. You bought it last season."

And when he said this, I had a fuzzy recollection of the card game, George Hamilton, and the rest. So we got the keys, went down, and checked it out. And you know what? George

Hamilton was right. It was terrific, a sweet little house with a pool and a view of the hills. We stayed there for twenty years.

Wherever you went with Sinatra, you were surrounded—by fans, by politicians, by celebrities, and yes, by mobsters. A lot has been made of this, but there was nothing much to it. If you were in show business, there really was no avoiding the Mafia. They were in the music industry, operated the nightclubs. They loved Frank, but they had no real place in his life. They came around for the same reason everyone else came around: because it was fun to be around Sinatra. The fact is, as much as these guys loved Sinatra, they loved Dino more. He was their guy, big and handsome and charming as hell. When it came to Dean, women would lie down and open their legs. It wasn't even a question of, "Should I?" "Maybe it's wrong?" They just did it. It was his manner, his way. He was Peck's bad boy. The gangsters swarmed around him. He worked as a blackjack dealer in the Beverly Hills Club in Cincinnati. Dean's whole philosophy was that everybody on the other side of the table is a sucker. Whoever he was dealing to was by definition a sucker. And when he got on stage, everybody in the audience was a sucker, too. That's why he sang the way he did, cocky and nonchalant—because he was singing to the suckers. He couldn't believe people actually paid to hear him.

Most of that mob stuff was just rumor or misunderstandings. I will tell you a story:

In the late seventies, I had a great idea for a show. Sinatra performing with Count Basie and Ella Fitzgerald. We would open on Broadway, then tour. We went through rehearsals, built sets, all the rest. Then, just before we were to open, word came down: The musicians are going to strike. The theater district will go dark. Did Sinatra care? Of course not. To him, it meant another night at 21. But for me, it was a disaster. I had a lot of my own money in the show. I would lose it all. I went around like a madman, meeting officials and union reps, trying to explain: *Look, we're not a Broadway show. We're a concert that is opening in a theater on Broadway. There's a difference. We should get an exemption from the strike.*

After twenty hours of this, I was sitting in a room outside the office of the union boss. I was spent, beat, wiped out, exhausted, undone, about to give it up. Just then, the door opens and out comes a woman, all done up, legs from here to here. She says, "Jerry? Jerry Weintraub?"

Uh-huh?

"Don't you recognize me, Jerry? I went to school with you. P.S. 70 in the Bronx."

"Oh, yeah," I say. "Of course, wow, you look fantastic!"

"I wish I could say the same about you. You're a mess. What's wrong?"

So I tell her the whole story—the show, the strike, how the show should not be part of the strike, and how a lot of the money in the show belongs to me, her friend from P.S. 70, Jerry Weintraub.

She takes me into the office of the union boss. He's not there. It's just me and her. She picks up the phone, makes a call. She gets the boss on the line. I can picture him, floating in his pool in Westchester or something, his wife and kids all around, his city-side honey suddenly ringing on the phone.

"I know you said don't call here, but I am sitting with an old friend from the Bronx, Jerry Weintraub, and what is happening to him and his show is just not fair... He needs an exemption... So I'm just gonna sign your name."

Which is how I walked out with that magic piece of paper.

The next day, the story was all over the tabloids: Look what Frank Sinatra has pulled off with his mob connections.

Sinatra was not without flaws. He was a human being, after all. He had his problems and insecurities like the rest of us. You had to monitor his mood. He was usually happy Rat Pack Sinatra, but sometimes he fell into a funk. You never really knew what you were going to get. Now and then, he suffered bleak, dark, low-down moods—you had to throw him a rope and haul him back to the surface. If you really cared about him—and I loved the guy, it should be obvious—you had to be prepared, on occasion, to pull him out of the hole.

So here's a story:

One day, I was at home, early in the morning, reading the paper, when the phone rang. It was Frank. Francis. He sounded down. He was calling from Vegas. It was 9:00 A.M. there. He had a regular gig at Caesars and was staying in a suite on top of the hotel. He never went to sleep before 6:00 or 7:00 A.M., which meant he had been up all night, drinking and brooding on the roof of the hotel, where he had his own swimming pool. Could I hear all this in his voice over the phone? Yes. My job is reading people, keeping them level, and, when necessary, hip-checking them back onto the sunlit track.

"You sound terrible," I said. "What's wrong?"

"Depressed, Jerry," he said. "Depressed."

"Why? What's going on?"

"I can't do it anymore," he said. "The same thing, every day and night, going down to that same theater and singing the same songs to the same crowds, 'Fly Me to the Moon,' 'Chicago,' I just don't care."

What was Frank? Sixty? Sixty-five? No, younger. Late fifties, but he seemed old to me, a man with a lifetime behind him. It was 1974. I was a kid. It was just the beginning. I got on a plane for Vegas that afternoon, took a cab to Caesars, sat on the roof, staring at the heat shimmers dancing over the flats. Frank talked. He had a drink in one hand, a smoke in the other, double fisted, his voice full of fatigue, but his eyes sparkled. He told me how unhappy he was, bored of this whole business of night after night and song after song.

"Maybe I need a rest," he said.

"It's not a rest you need," I told him. "It's a new hill to climb."

This was Frank's nature. He was at his best when he was battling, fighting, struggling against all those fools who told him he had bitten off too much, gone too far. "You're bored," I explained. "You need a challenge."

"All right," he said, "what do you have in mind?"

"I have a great idea," I told him, "but I don't want to talk about it until I've had time to really put it together."

"No, no, what is it?" he asked. "You've got to tell me."

I said, "Look, I really do have a great idea, but I need a few days."

Of course, I did not have a great idea. I had no idea at all, but I knew that Frank needed a great idea less than he needed the prospect of a great idea, the promise of an event that would lift him out of his funk.

He said, "Tell me, Jerry. You've got to tell me."

So I started talking, improvising...

"Were going to do Madison Square Garden," I said.

"Yeah, so what?" said Frank. "We've done Madison Square Garden before. What's so great about that?"

"Now wait, Frank, hold on, let me tell you how we're going to do it…"

I kicked my voice up a notch, going into full ringmaster mode.

"…We're going to do it live, Frank! *Live!*"

"Yeah, so what? We're live every night. That's show business."

"Yes, but we're never live like this," I said, "on every television in America and all across the world."

"Yeah?"

"Yeah…"

And now that I had gotten the thread I was gone.

"And let's do it in the center of the Garden," I told him, "on the floor, in a boxing ring."

"A boxing ring? What are you talking about?"

"I'll tell you what I'm talking about. You're the heavyweight champion of the world, Frank. You hold every belt in the world of entertainment. The number-one singer in the world. No challengers, no one even close. So let's do it in a ring, and make it like a heavyweight title fight, and invite all the people who go to heavyweight title fights, because they're your fans. And let's get Howard Cosell to be the announcer. Yeah, wow, I can hear it!"

"Hear what, Jerry? What can you hear?"

"I can hear Howard Cosell. He's ringside, his hand over his ear, announcing it as you come down the aisle, climb through the ropes and into the ring: "Ladies and gentlemen, live from Madison Square Garden. Jerry Weintraub presents 'Sinatra, the Main Event.'

"And here's the best part," I told Frank. "No rehearsals."

"No rehearsals."

"No rehearsals. You just get there on the night of the show, and sing your songs, and do your thing, as fresh and spontaneous as can be—like a heavyweight title fight. Frank Sinatra Live!"

"The Main Event" was one of the great concert events of the age, Sinatra, in a ring in the center of his town, singing the story of his life, and this is how it began, on the roof of Caesars, Sinatra depressed and brooding, Weintraub talking and talking.

When we got to New York, Sinatra checked into a suite in the Waldorf Astoria and I went to the Garden to set this thing up. *Live? In every house in America, in every nation on earth? What was I thinking?* The project had grown quickly—too quickly. It started as a concert broadcast on TV, but there was now a record and a film. And we had five days to pull it off. Just like that, I had three hundred people working for me. By the second day, I was feeling pressure. By the fourth, I was in a mild panic. By the fifth, I was out of my mind. What had started as a ploy to snap Frank out of his depression had turned into a major deal—handled wrong, it could turn into a major embarrassment.

At such times, I become obsessed with details. That's where God is, so that's where I go, with my notebook and phone numbers and head full of ideas. The people, the angles, the chairs—I wanted to get everything exactly right. I hired Roone Arledge, who was then head of ABC Sports and ABC News, to produce the broadcast. I hired Don Ohlmeyer, who ended up being president of NBC, and Dick Ebersol, who later ran NBC Sports, and still does.

We built the boxing ring, arranged the seats, rehearsed the camera moves, intros, and exits, everything choreographed to a fraction of a second. Commercials were a major issue. We were supposed to break six times in the hour, and needed a system whereby Frank would know when to close out a song and when to start back in. Also, which songs would work the best as hooks, and which would work the best as lead-ins to new segments. Simply put, I needed Frank at the Garden for a rehearsal. But when I called his room at the Waldorf, there was no answer, nor a return call, day after day. Finally, on the morning of the show, a secretary answered.

"This is Jerry Weintraub," I told her. "I've got to talk to Frank."

"I'm sorry," she said. "Mr. Sinatra is not available."

"What the hell are you talking about?" I said. "We have a show tonight! At 8:00 P.M., we go live around the world."

"I'm sorry," she said "but he's indisposed."

Click.

I kept calling, but he never got on the phone.

At 2:00 P.M. a note arrived from Sinatra. It was his set list, the songs he planned to sing. It was ridiculous, absurd. I could not believe what was on there. "Crocodile Rock," "Disco Inferno."

To hell with this! I jump in a cab and head over to the Waldorf.

I went through the lobby, up the elevator, knocked on the door. I was in a panic. Clearly, Sinatra was not. He was, in fact, sitting in his bathrobe, smoking a cigarette as he read the newspaper. I went over, holding the set list.

"What is this?" I asked.

"What's what?" he said.

"These songs."

He laughed. His hair was pushed back and every part of him glittered. His funk had clearly lifted. "Forget the list," he said.

"I wanted to see you, and figured that list would get you here quicker than a phone call."

"Okay, great," I said, "why did you want to see me?"

"Because you've been calling every eight minutes. What do you need, Jerry?"

"Well, I'll tell you," I said. "We have a live show in five hours, Frank. I need you to come to the Garden."

"No, Jerry, you said no rehearsal, remember? Live?"

"Yeah, I remember, but this thing has grown."

"Don't worry, Jerry."

Sinatra obviously had a plan in mind, but he was not sharing it with me.

"Well, I am worried," I said. "Can't we just do a quick run-through?"

"No, Jerry, no rehearsal. That's what you said. I will be there when the show starts. That's when you need me. Not before."

At 7:30 P.M., his limo pulled into Madison Square Garden. The streets were filled with scalpers and fans—and that special electricity only Frank could generate. He had arrived with a police escort, sirens, flashing lights. He climbed out, straightened his tux, tossed away a cigarette, took my arm, and asked, "How you doing, kid?"

"Not great," I said.

"We'll fix that in a minute," he told me. "First, remember to tell your wife, Jane, to get in the car when I start singing 'My Way.' I want to go by Patsy's and pick up some pizzas for the plane."

So that was what he was thinking about—not the show, not

the commercial breaks, not the slender thread that was holding me above the flames of oblivion, but the pizzas he would eat on the way back to Palm Springs.

As we were walking to the dressing room, his entourage trailing behind us, he said, "Okay, Jerry. What's the problem?"

"We're going to commercial six times in this hour," I told him, "and this is a live show, and you don't know when to break."

"Jerry, is there a kid around here with a red jacket?" he asked.

"I'm sure we can get one," I said. "Why?"

"Have a kid in a red coat stand up ringside with a sign that says 'five minutes,'" he said. "When I see him, I will start 'My Way.'"

"Okay," I said, "but what are you going to do during the six commercial breaks?"

He said, "I'm going to sing, Jerry. That's what I am going to do. When you go to commercial, I will be singing and when you come back, I will still be singing. That's live."

He taught me about spontaneity that night—this, too, helped me as a film producer. Live, let it happen. There's never a better take than the first: Sinatra knew that in his bones.

If you watch a tape of the "Main Event," you see me and Sinatra walk out of the dressing room and down the aisle side by side. He is Muhammad Ali and I am Cus D'Amato, the trainer, the cut man, the voice in the ear, saying, "You are the champ! It's yours! Now get in there and murder the bum!" I was, in fact, as white as a sheet, shuffling as if to my own funeral. You hear Cosell going though his routine: "... Here, coming through the same tunnel that so many champions have walked before, the great man, Frank Sinatra, who has the phrasing, who has the control, who knows what losing means, who made the great comeback, and now stands still, eternally, on top of the entertainment world..." Just before we went out, when the music started Sinatra leaned over me—well, I was a lot taller than Frank, so he looked up, but it felt like he was leaning over me, you know? And he asked, "How you doing now? Better?"

"No," I said, "not better."

"What the hell's the matter with you?" he said.

"Frank"—or Francis, that's what I said—"this is going live around the world, we have not rehearsed and have no markers or breaks. It could be the end of my career."

He pinched my cheek and said, "Listen, kid. You got me into this, and I'm going to get you out."

And he went through the ropes, and the music started, and it was all Frank from there. He was a genius. He held the crowd in his hand. "The Lady Is a Tramp," "Angel Eyes," "My Kind of Town," they poured out of him like Norse sagas. When he sang "Autumn in New York," it was as if he were leaning on a bar, spilling his guts out to a late-night, Hopperesque bartender.

Who thought this could work, intimacy in an arena filled with thousands and thousands of people, but he pulled it off. He turned the Garden into a shadowy, three-in-the-morning, Second Avenue saloon. You could have heard a pin drop.

Then, just like that, when it seemed no more than a moment had passed, the kid walked the aisle in the red coat and Frank launched into "My Way." The ignition was turned in the limo, the pizzas were pulled from the ovens, the plane raced down the runway, and we were laughing and eating pepperoni as the jet climbed into the stratosphere.

Sam and Rose Weintraub, my parents.

Me and Melvyn, on the day I became a man (meaning, my Bar Mitzvah).

In uniform, down South.

Jane Morgan, great love, mentor, and friend, in the hit record years soon after we first met.

What's that great old Sinatra tune? "When the World Was Young"!

Congressman Kennedy. I was in love with the man the moment I met him. Can't you tell?

Walter Winchell, the legendary gossip columnist, looking at Jane in a manner not entirely kosher as I smile for the camera.

Elvis said, "You knew John Kennedy? Well, hey, I know politicians too!" Then proved it by setting up this meeting: me, the Colonel, the Memphis Mafia, George Wallace (seated), Mrs. Wallace, and Elvis (not seated).

A great buddy picture: the Colonel and me on the road with the King!

If you're going to stand in an icy river, you might as well drink a beer. Me and John Denver in the golden years.

Me in red, Bernie Brillstein in blue, and that guy in the middle, I think his name was Belushi.

My son, Michael, one of my best friends.

The family, left to right: Jamie, Jerry, Julie, Jody, and Jane.

Armand Hammer and I in Red Square with the coffin of Leonid Brezhnev. I said, "Hey Armand, why are you smiling? Your friend just died."

Armand Hammer and I talk business with Yitzhak Shamir, the prime minister of Israel.

Cheer up Jerry!
Have a good time!
love
Francis

Here I am with Professor Sinatra who taught me about timing—the key to everything.

Sometimes you just need a good soak.

With Cary Grant, who was as good as they get.

Here I am with the president, attending to matters of state.

On the set of *The Karate Kid, Part II*: me, Pat Morita, Barbara Bush, John Avildsen, President Bush, and Ralph Macchio. (*Ralph Nelson SMPSP*)

Best seat in the house. (*Phil Caruso*)

Taking direction from Sydney Pollock in *The Firm*, as Gene Hackman and Tom Cruise look on. It ain't easy working with a novice! (*François Duhamel*)

A great honor: worshipping alongside Rebbe Schneerson in Brooklyn.

Bruce Willis and me, overdressed but still happy. (*Alex J. Berliner* ©
Berliner Studio/BEImages)

Some choice words from George Clooney on the set of *Ocean's Eleven*. (*Bob Marshak*)

Matt Damon about to get me with the old, "Hey, there's something on your shirt" trick. (*Alex J. Berliner © Berliner Studio/BEImages*)

Brad Pitt hanging out with the sexiest man alive. (*Melinda Sue Gordon*)

On the set of *Ocean's Twelve* in Amsterdam. Friends are what counts. (*Ralph Nelson SMPSP*)

Steven Soderbergh being typically patient with his producer. (*Ralph Nelson SMPSP*)

Jerry – Big love to you! Julia

With Julia Roberts. (*Bob Marshak*)

Putting my prints in the wet cement, with Brad, George, and Matt. Great day. (*David Hume Kennerly*)

Susie and me...there is a Sinatra song about this sort of thing too! (*Norman Jean Roy*)

Firing Ferguson

Around this time, in 1978, Jane and I purchased land in Malibu and built the house where she still spends much of the year. I describe it as a beach shack, but it really is one of the great California houses, a compound more than a house, with stables and guest quarters and trails that run across six acres on the Pacific coast, where the land juts out and Catalina Island rises into view. If you leave Beverly Hills at 2:00 P.M., heading north on the Pacific Coast Highway, with the sea on your left and the hills rising steeply on your right, you will arrive before three, finally passing through a gate marked "Blue Heaven."

In the midseventies, Jane and I threw a lot of parties. She calls it the era of "extreme entertaining." We had people over most nights, the rooms filled with music and movie types, the windows glittering, laughter spilling onto the beach, where I stand with a bottle of wine knee deep in the surf. In the garage in Malibu, we have posterboard-size pictures taken in those bygone days. Jane with Walter Winchell. Jane with Darryl Zanuck and John Wayne. Jane, at a dinner party, with three different kinds of crystal in front of her, seated between Frank Sinatra and Cary Grant.

By then, my touring company, Concerts West, was booming. But no matter how well I was doing, I was always on the lookout for the new artist, the next big thing. When I think back on those years, it's me going from club to club, sitting at cocktail tables, meeting artists in cramped dressing rooms, pitching, cajoling, selling. (Breaking a new act is a special high; some agents spend their careers chasing it.) My most noteworthy find of those years was John Denver, who, as far as I am concerned, I cooked from scratch. By examining how I dealt with John Denver you can get a pretty good sense of the task and challenge of the manager, how he finds and builds an act, and how that act will eventually break his heart.

John was a military brat. His childhood was spent moving base to base, New Mexico, Arizona, Alabama, Texas. His real name was John Deutschendorf Jr. His father was an amazing guy, a test pilot and flight instructor who often seemed confused by his kid. The love of music and songwriting, the long hair and pursuit of beauty—where did they come from? John left home as soon as he was of age. He traveled the country with a guitar and a notebook of songs. He was going to write about everything, all of it, the mountains and plains, the continental divide, set it to music. He made a few solo records, which went nowhere, then scored one big success, "Leaving on a Jet Plane," which went top ten when recorded by Peter, Paul, and Mary, who, by the way, I managed. But his first real break came in the midsixties, when, answering an open audition, he won a spot in the Chad Mitchell Trio, a hot New York folk act.

I first heard about John when he left the Trio and was

looking to make it on his own. He had been represented by Irwin Winkler, who was going into the movie business, and needed representation. A friend tipped me: "Jerry, check out this kid. He's playing a dive in Greenwich Village." So I went over. No one there. The joint was empty. Just this earnest kid with a pageboy haircut, singing and playing guitar on stage. I sat and listened. He made a connection immediately. That's how it was with him—his talent. With each song, you felt he had opened his chest and was showing you his beating heart.

Okay, you might think, Jerry Weintraub and John Denver, something does not compute, something is not right. How does a folk singer from New Mexico end up in league with a street kid from the Bronx? But the fact is, we were a lot alike, me and John, had a lot in common, which is why our friendship was so immediate and deep. He, too, had run away from home when he was a kid—he left in his father's car and turned up weeks later at a cousin's house in Los Angeles. He, too, wanted to get out into the world, see and experience everything, find his way. I saw all of this that first night in New York. I saw the talent, too. It was one of those rare moments you dream of as a manager— spotting the kid who will become a star, who is a star already, even if the world does not yet know it.

From that moment, I was determined to break John Denver. He would be a test case for all my theories on selling and packaging, for everything I had learned since I left home and before, on the streets in the Bronx and from my father. John Denver would be my Star of Ardaban.

I wanted to start by getting some noise going. Here was this gem, John Denver, playing five nights a week in Greenwich Village, virtually for free—he was making seventy dollars a show when I met him—and no one even knew it. I went all around New York and LA, talking my head off to all the big operators. *John Denver. Have you seen this kid? John Denver. He's amazing. John Denver.* I went on like this until my friends said, "All right. We get it! John Denver. Shut up."

"Shut up about who?"

"John Denver."

"Yeah, isn't he great?"

Then I started to embroider, embellish. I would say, "Wow, John Denver, this client of mine, he's so great, so on fire, that Bob Dylan has been hanging out in this club every night, watching him play."

Just get them there, that's what I believed. Just get them there, let them see this kid, they will love him.

Did it work?

Of course it did.

Within a few weeks, the place in the Village was packed, every seat filled, and the patrons three deep at the bar.

"Okay," I said, "now let us see what we can do about this seventy dollars a night nonsense."

John had cut a record for RCA. This was part of his long-term contract. He had already made *Rhymes and Reasons* and *Take Me to Tomorrow*. This was all before I got there—pre-Jerry. The new record was called *Poems, Prayers and Promises*. It had one obvious hit: "Take Me Home, Country Roads." But the challenge was the same as always: get people to hear it, to recognize it as a hit. This mirrors the greater challenge of the talent manager. I did not invent John Denver. I did not write his hits, or create anything that was not there before I arrived. No manager does that. As I tell aspiring agents and managers, remember where the engine lies: with the artist. If the artist makes nothing, I have nothing to sell. It's as simple as that.

It's best, when selling something new, to envision the goal—let the entire world hear John Denver—then work your way back. How do we get there? Now and then, it happens by itself. This is a matter of luck, zeitgeist. More often, you have to be creative, crabwalk your way. Once the new record was released, I sent John on a tour of the biggest radio stations in the country. He would turn up by himself, with his song and his guitar, as if he just stumbled out of the mountains.

You have to remember what John looked like back then. He was simple and blond with the bangs and the glasses. This was the early seventies, when everyone was looking for his own Jimmy Carter, a man he could trust. John, with his apple-pie face, was perfectly cast. He came to hate this, but he was lucky. He had just what the market was demanding. It was his trademark, as the blue suede shoes and pompadour trademarked Elvis. It was his thing. You can evolve and grow but you should never resent your thing. If you look at how few artists actually make it, you will recognize that those trademarks, though in some ways limiting, are a gift of providence. John would show up with his pageboy and all-American smile and say, "Hi, I'm John Denver. I would like to play a song for you." And bang, he was on the air.

At times, I used my other clients to break John. Fame is a private party. You can dazzle your way in with talent, or you can be vouched for. How far this can be carried depends entirely on who is doing the vouching. If it's Frankie Valli, okay, maybe. But if it's Sinatra? I arranged for John to cross paths with Elvis on the road. They went to radio stations, or Elvis mentioned one of John's songs. I had learned something important from the incident of the unsold scarves. A mention by Elvis was the same as a multimillion-dollar ad campaign.

I had Sinatra talk about John, hook up with John, be seen with John. You might think of Sinatra and Denver as a mismatch (like Weintraub and Denver; like martinis and moonshine) but everything blurred in the seventies—this is when Sinatra recorded "(It's Not Easy) Bein' Green." It was an odd moment, and yet another lesson for producers and managers: know your age, sing its songs. If you cross-breed the Elvis audience with the Sinatra audience, you get the great big everyone the Colonel spent his life chasing. We were not interested in niche marketing, or in targeting a selected demographic: We wanted them all.

Soon after its release, "Country Roads" was dominating the charts. You could not turn on your radio without hearing it.

The song, the tour, the public appearances—these were means to an end, which was not merely to have a hit, but to turn John into a star: not a star in prospect, but a star now and yesterday, someone who has already happened, so accomplished it's no longer up for debate. It's why I did not present John Denver as an exciting find, or as someone who had recently been playing to an empty house in Greenwich Village, but as talent that had already made it, an accomplished fact. I sold him in the past tense, as someone you've known about for years. I was telling the audience to relax and enjoy, as the judgment has already been made. *You love him!* In this way, we skipped several steps, jumping directly from the early days of struggle to the golden years.

I bought every billboard on Sunset Boulevard from Bel Air to Hollywood. On each, I put a different picture of John, a different posture, a different mood. You could not drive to work without being bombarded. He was all over the place. By the time you heard his song, you already knew him. I met with executives at RCA. They wanted to cut a follow-up to *Poems, Prayers and Promises*. I convinced them to do a greatest-hits album, which was amazing, considering John only had one hit. This is what I mean by selling John as if he were already a star. They paid us a million dollars for the record—a huge sum in those days. It came out in 1977, went straight to the top of the charts, and stayed there.

We branched out from there, transitioning John to TV. Within a few years, he was almost as well known for his work on the small screen as he was for his songs. He made his first appearance on *The Tonight Show* in 1972. I was friends with Johnny Carson and hooked them up at a party at my house in Beverly Hills. John became a regular on *The Tonight Show*, appearing again and again. America was still one market, and Carson stood at the center of it—it's hard to explain just what a big deal that show was. Then, one summer, when Carson went on vacation, the producer asked John to fill in as guest host. It was a milestone for any entertainer—like the moment the mob takes you into a basement with the wood paneling and makes you swear loyalty over a book. You're a made man after that, untouchable.

In 1974, I signed a deal with ABC under which John would do five guest spots on various network shows, getting paid $2,500 an appearance. In the end, ABC only used him once, in a Chevy Special, then called and canceled the rest of the contract. In other words, they dropped him. Four weeks later, "Country Roads" hit. A few weeks after that, I signed a new deal with ABC, under which he would be paid $350,000 an appearance. Remember, when I found John, he was playing in the

Village for seventy bucks a night. What happened to him, the way he blew up, was amazing.

John understood all this, and appreciated it. He paid me a fortune. There were many years in which I made ten, twelve million with John. But for me, the money was a by-product of what was a labor of love. I had many clients, some of them bigger than John—Elvis and Frank, Neil Diamond, Bob Dylan— but John and I were very close. Because I broke him, because I understood him, because he understood me, because I loved him. We started as friends but became brothers. He made me the executor of his estate, he was executor of mine. Jane and I were to take care of his children if, God forbid, anything were to happen to him and his wife, Annie.

Yet there was something troubled about John. Success and money, rather than making these things easier to deal with, often bring them to the surface. He had an overwhelming need to impress and be accepted. It probably came from his father and the fact that John never seemed to win his approval, even when he made it big. He was in search of a father, really, someone who could stand in the old man's place and say, "Yes, John, I love you. Yes." And though he wanted a father and wanted approval, he resented the fact that he wanted those things. He needed you to love him, and hated you for making him feel that need. This sowed dangerous seeds in our relationship. After all, who was I? The man in the suit who paid the bills and made the schedule. In other words, I was the father. As he became more successful, he began to resent me. He needed me, but hated me for that need. I understood this only later.

John was beloved by fans but never accepted by critics, and it drove him crazy. No matter how many records he sold, no matter how much adulation was showered on him, he needed to win and be loved by the people who had already made up their minds, who thought he was lightweight and silly. I would say, "Hey, John, who gives a crap?" Or: "You know what? Screw 'em." If you want to survive, if you want a long life and career, if you want to go wire to wire and have a decent time doing it, you need to have a deep strain of "Screw 'em." I would say, "Believe me, John, you're better with the people than with the critics. That counts if you're an actor, a producer, a politician, or a singer."

But he could not let it go. The criticism drove him wild. He was troubled, as I said. He had no identity. He didn't know what he wanted because he did not know who he was. He wanted to ditch his glasses for contact lenses. "But the glasses are part of the shtick," I told him. "The glasses are great!" I mean, if you're getting hitters out with screwballs, keep throwing the screwballs. That's the sportsman's way.

The first danger sign came in 1979, when John was on tour in Europe. I got a call from one of my assistants on the road. "John is unhappy," he said. "He's talking about firing you."

I got on a plane, went over. I stood with John outside the Inn on the Park in London. He had his head down and paced, the way he did whenever faced with an onerous task or crisis. He stammered. He said, "Look, Jerry. You know how I feel about our relationship, but I think I am going to have to let you go."

"Let me go? Why?"

"Well, it's this tour. I mean, nothing is right. The hotels stink, and the food is no good, and the venues are just awful, and the sound systems are terrible, too. The band is furious. Nothing is right."

I said, "Look, I just got off a flight from LA. Let me get some rest. Then let's talk it over in four hours."

"What's going to happen in four hours?" he asked.

"Well, maybe I can fix these problems," I said. "Think of all we've been through. You can give me four hours."

"All right," he said, "four hours, but I am deadly serious, Jerry."

"I know you are, John."

That night, we went out to dinner after his show.

I said, "Look, John. Before we eat, I want you to know I've taken care of the problem. Things will be different from here."

"You took care of them? How?"

"I fired Ferguson."

"You fired Ferguson? Who's Ferguson?"

"There has been trouble with the hotels, with the food, with the venues, with the sound systems? Well, Ferguson was in charge of all of that. He's been fired."

"Really? You fired Ferguson."

"I did. And I think you will notice the difference right away."

We started eating, talking, being brothers again. I was brooding, looking down.

"What's the matter, Jerry?"

"Well, I'll tell you, John. I'm feeling bad about Ferguson. Sure, he screwed up, but he's not a terrible guy. And now he's been fired, and he won't have his salary and he won't have his bonus and it's right before Christmas. For godsakes, John, Ferguson has a family!"

We sat in silence, eating. Finally, John threw down his napkin and said, "Darn it, I feel bad about Ferguson, too!"

Some time went by. I was eating, drinking, looking around. It was one of those stolid British restaurants, with brass on everything and waiters coming and going with pints of ale.

I said, "Look, I have an idea. Let's say, instead of firing

Ferguson, I just move him into another part of the business. Away from people."

"Hide him, you mean?"

"Yeah, hide him. In the business, just not out front, definitely not working with artists."

"Yeah, that's a great idea," said John. "I would feel a lot better about that, it being so close to Christmas and all."

"Good," I said. "I will call LA tomorrow and take care of it. Ferguson's wife is going to be so relieved."

There really was nothing wrong with the hotels, food, venues, or the rest. John had just gotten himself in a tangle and needed to stand up for himself. Which was why we fired Ferguson. I also knew that John was very compassionate and would eventually blame himself for what happened to Ferguson, which was why we hired him back.

The next night, on the way back from the show, I asked John, "So how was the venue, how was the sound?"

"Oh, much better," he said. "I could tell the difference right away. I'm glad we could fix it without firing Ferguson."

Of course, there was no Ferguson.

Jerry Weintraub Presents

B y this time, Concerts West had become perhaps the most important company in the industry, known for its live shows and productions. John Denver was just one of many talented artists who made me a force. I did not handle all these people personally—I had partners, employees—but I was sitting over everything, experiencing the entire scene.

I loved and appreciated all my artists, and still do. There was, for example, Bob Dylan. He was a god to his fans, but to me he was just another smart, Jewish kid from the provinces. Yes, he is brilliant. I don't think he has any idea just how brilliant. The man can break your heart with a turn of phrase. But to him it is just another day of work, which is how I treated it, too. Not even a priest wants to be revered when he's away from the church. He wants to go home and have a drink, knowing the lights will stay on and the bills will be paid. And that was my job. After all, an artist like Dylan has enough fans. A man to mind the store, to keep the books, that's what he needs.

And then there was Led Zeppelin, who we signed in the midseventies. Once you start working with the Presleys and Sinatras, other people, the superstars and up-and-comers, come looking for you. It's called momentum, what people mean by the phrase "cooking with gas."

"Jerry Weintraub?"

"Yeah?"

"You've got to help me!"

"Why?"

"Because I've got dreams!"

"All right, my boy! All right."

Zeppelin was wild. Our first concert with them was at Nassau Coliseum on Long Island. They were bitching after the show about the sound system: It did not have enough channels, not enough speakers, blah, blah. It was so loud the place was shaking. I was worried about a cave-in or structural disaster. But no, they wanted bigger, louder, more decibels, more, more, more. When these guys played "Stairway to Heaven," they wanted to build an actual stairway to heaven. The next day, I went around with a few of my guys and gathered every box on the island. We painted them black. I can still smell the fumes from the spray-paint. They made me high. We brought the boxes to the Coliseum and stacked them in huge piles on either side of the stage, hundreds of these goddamn things.

"What the hell are these, Jerry?"

"What do they look like? They're the goddamn speakers, schmuck. You want loud, you're gonna have loud."

That night, Zeppelin exploded onto the stage as if they'd been shot from a cannon, like clowns at the circus, danced and screamed and made a lot of wonderful noise, reveling in the mighty power of this wall of speakers, which, of course, were not connected to anything. If you expect loud, loud is what you are going to hear.

A lot of the time, these guys made demands just to be

demanding. These were rock stars. They needed to say "Screw you!" to whoever was cutting the check or wearing the suit. It's part of the job description.

One afternoon, before Zeppelin was scheduled to play at Madison Square Garden, I went into a men's store on Fifth Avenue and picked up a gorgeous suit that had been tailor-made for me in London. I tried it on for the mirror—hand-stitched, double-breasted, beautiful—put it in a bag, and carried it to the arena, where I hung it in a closet in the dressing room, with a note pinned on the front: WEINTRAUB! HANDS OFF!

I went out front to watch the show. The lights went down, the announcer spoke over the sound system: "Now, the loudest, most dangerous rock band on earth…" The crowd went nuts, Zeppelin came on stage. Jimmy Page, John Paul Jones, Robert Plant. John Bonham, the drummer, came out last. He was wearing whatever crap those guys wore, but over it he had on a beautiful blue jacket.

What the hell?

He sat behind the drums, then, in one clean motion, ripped off the sleeves so you could see his arms and shouted, "How do I look, Jerry Weintraub? I've got your new suit." He held up the arms of the suit, then launched into "Black Dog."

It was hysterical.

For years, I handled the Moody Blues, a British group that went through various incarnations before breaking through in 1965 with the song "Go Now." (They are best known for "Nights in White Satin" and "Tuesday Afternoon.") I had a brilliant pitch for these guys: I sold them as everyone's second-favorite band. *Are you a Beatles freak? Well, you're going to love the Moodies second. Are the Stones your thing? Great! Then check out the Moodies. You'll like them almost as much.* We made a lot of money with that. We were, in essence, harvesting several fields at once, collecting everyone's runoff. Then these guys did a stupid thing. They broke up. It always happens. The more successful a band, the more certain its demise, as each member gets to thinking, "Well, it's because of me, it's my success, and I'm tired of sharing it."

Two of the Moodies, Justin Hayward and John Lodge, calling themselves the Blue Jays, decided to make their own record. I tried to talk sense. "We've spent years positioning the Moody Blues, and, as a result, millions and millions of people consider you their second-favorite band," I explained, "but no one has heard of the Blue Jays. You'll be starting from scratch."

Did they care?

Of course not.

When I could see they had made up their minds, I decided to get on board, pitch in. For me, the challenge was plain: get people to judge these veteran rock stars as if they were new, notice, and take time. Convincing cynical members of the establishment to rethink something they believe they already know is no small thing. You might call it a relaunch, or rebranding, but it really just amounts to a man from the Bronx yelling: *Here, here, look over here! Remember this? It's still really good!* They worked on their album for a year. When it was finished, I had beautiful invitations printed and carried by courier, with great pomp and circumstance, to journalists and critics all across the country. They read like tickets to an exclusive, impossible-to-get-into, one-time-only show by the geniuses behind your second-favorite band—Justin Hayward and John Lodge, playing at Carnegie Hall in New York City.

Critics and producers and celebrities turned up from all over the world. The show was in the afternoon. They took their seats. You could feel a tremendous buzz as the lights went down. Everyone was excited. But when the curtain came up, instead of rock stars and their band, there was just a huge, fantastic sound system. You could see tremendous speakers, but no band. Then I played the record, from start to finish. All along, people were yelling, "Down in front! I can't see!" But there was nothing to see, just all the hardware. I wanted to play the songs—I wanted these people, these influential people, to sit and listen to them, really listen, as the record unfolded. Yes, I could have had the Blue Jays perform (they would have been great), but the critics knew Hayward and Lodge, or thought they did. They would watch the show, like it or not like it, and move on. But this night, with that record playing on stage, well, they would never forget it. Some would denounce me, sure, but, with each denunciation, they would mention the record and the band.

I held a press conference after the show. The critics filled the room. They were furious. Jann Wenner, the owner and editor of *Rolling Stone*, and a great guy, was the first to speak. "You, sir, are a charlatan," he said. He was red with anger. "You have tricked these people with a stunt, made them come all this way, and for what? To sit and listen to a record? They could have done that at home and saved the money and time and fuel. You are P. T. Barnum."

"Okay, okay," I said, trying to calm everyone down. "You've had your say. Now let me have mine—after that, call me whatever you want. The fact is," I explained, "we've spent an entire year of our lives working on this record, and we're proud of it, and think it deserves to be heard, really heard. So what are we supposed to do? Send it to your house so you can put it on the record player? Well, maybe your stereo stinks and the sound stinks, and maybe you had a fight with your wife, and maybe your baby puked on you. So it plays, but it does not get heard.

Well, now you have heard it. So go home and say whatever you want about me, but remember the effort that went into this record."

Rolling Stone ran an editorial about the show. It filled half a page. I was called many terrible names, but, in the end, they said, well, you know, he kind of has a point.

We were remaking the concert business in those years. Starting with Elvis, we took an industry that had been regional, divided among fiefdoms, with each territory controlled by a single promoter, and made it national. In the process, we cut out the middlemen. It was just me and the artist, working as partners, cutting deals directly with the owners of concert halls. Costs fell, everyone was enriched. As a result, artists sought me out, wanting to cut the same deal. Which increased my power. I was now able to go to the owner of Madison Square Garden and say, for example, "I'm going to give you thirty nights of shows this year—what kind of break can you give me on the hall?" In this way, overhead fell, and, as overhead fell, profits rose, attracting still more artists, which meant still more dates, which meant still better deals, which meant still more profits, and so on.

Remember how I said everyone was enriched by this process? Well, that is not exactly true. The fact is, when my business took off, the men who ran the old system, the promoters and operators, first got squeezed, then went under. In the academy, they call it creative destruction. I had invented a newer, more efficient model, which meant the old model was doomed. On the street, they call it pain.

The old promoters and middlemen grew to resent me. I was their bogeyman, *the* devil. The table is covered with settings and piled with food, and here comes Weintraub to pull out the cloth. They called a big meeting on Long Island. (I don't remember the exact year.) You want to feel persecuted? Imagine dozens of record men boarding planes all across the country with a single goal in mind: putting you out of business. The meeting was organized by Frank Barcelona, an agent with a personal beef. He represented Zeppelin. When I made the pitch to promote the band, I went around him, directly to their lawyer—Steve Weiss—who cut a side deal with us, which was a tremendous threat to Barcelona. (Zeppelin was real money.)

The charge against me went like this: "Weintraub doesn't build artists. The local managers and promoters build artists, then Weintraub swoops in and takes them away."

Here's how San Francisco's Bill Graham, the biggest independent promoter in America at the time, explained it to *Newsweek*: "Jerry Weintraub comes into town like an eagle, scoops up the money, and leaves. He tells his acts, 'For a piece of the action, I can eliminate certain promoters and agents.' He's more a power broker than a producer."

My answer? Well, hell, yes, of course that's what I do. It's called business. Why do you think I'm successful?

(Bill Graham and I were great friends before this, and we remained great friends.)

I don't really know what came out of this meeting other than a bunch of chatter. The fact is, if a bunch of men are discussing you, meeting about you, and scheming to destroy you, it probably means you're doing something right.

In those years, my key relationship was with the owners of the arenas. That's where I cut my deals and made my profit. The owners were a unique breed, almost entirely gone now, wheelers and dealers, big-money boys, political players, sharpies and sharks, the makers and builders of cities. It was not art or ideas that interested these men. It was bricks and mortar, seats, stages, real estate. A few of them became my teachers. Here I am thinking mostly of Arthur Wirtz, who owned the Chicago Stadium and was one of the truly interesting people of his era.

For a long time, Arthur Wirtz was just a name, like John Doe is a name—I had heard it, but I was not sure where and not sure why. I took an interest only when I started making my way in the concert business. I had two or three months' worth of shows a year and was looking to strike a deal in Chicago, that fantastic market. Chicago Stadium was the obvious place. It had about twenty thousand seats, which is as big as you get before you have to move outside. Other than the Bulls, the Blackhawks, the Ice Capades, and the Circus, which adds up to about a hundred nights a year, the place stood empty.

I went to Chicago and started asking around.

"Who do I have to talk to cut a deal on the Stadium?"

Arthur Wirtz, you've got to talk to Arthur Wirtz.

Arthur Wirtz was huge, six-foot-six, with gray hair. He wore wire-framed glasses, an odd, dandified touch on an otherwise classic Chicago face. He had been to college, but kept something of the street about him, the grit of the west side club rooms. He was like a boss in an old movie, a mountain of a man behind a desk, the city humming behind him—Chicago, with its steel towers and slaughter yards. He had fought his way to the top of a tough town, and I admired him. He made his first fortune in commercial real estate, but his true talent had always been sales. Sell, earn, invest, increase. His family still owns the Blackhawks. He began to acquire things, which is how an ordinary man becomes a titan. By the time I started asking around,

Wirtz had become a power in Chicago, the man behind the aldermen, the man behind the mayor.

Though sensible and hard-nosed, he had an eye for showbiz. He built the stadium, then needed to fill the seats. He owned an NHL franchise. It did so well he acquired interests in several others. He came to own most of the teams in the league, including franchises in Montreal, Toronto, and Detroit. He also brought Sonja Henie to America and produced her ice shows, which led to the Ice Capades. He was a giant.

"I don't understand Arthur Wirtz," I told a Chicago friend. "Why doesn't he put other shows in the Stadium?"

"He doesn't want other shows," my friend told me. "He has the Ice Capades, he has the circus, hockey, and basketball. He doesn't know from anything else."

I called Wirtz's office and left a message. No return. I called again. Nothing. It was like shouting into a well. Nothing came back.

Around this time, I ran into Bob Strauss, from Texas. He was a big player in the Democratic Party. I asked him if he could help set up a meeting with Arthur Wirtz. He laughed.

"What's so funny?" I asked.

"You can't just meet with a man like Wirtz," he told me.

"Well, then, how the hell am I supposed to do business with him?"

"You have to talk to Mayor Daley's people first," he told me. "You can't do anything in Chicago without the machine."

"Great, set up a meeting with Daley."

"No, no, no," said Bob, laughing. "You don't actually meet with Daley. You meet with Colonel Riley."

"Colonel Riley? Who the hell is Colonel Riley?"

"Everything in Chicago goes through Daley," he explained, "and everything that goes through Daley goes through Colonel Riley. You meet with him, work it out, then you get to meet with Wirtz."

"Work what out?"

"Just meet him."

I met Colonel Riley in the Bismarck Hotel across from City Hall. This is where the operators and aldermen hung out, where deals got done. We took a table in back. The Colonel hung his jacket on the back of his chair. It was nine in the morning, but the place was filled with newspapermen, union leaders, tough guys, and such. Riley was a skinny Irishman with a patch over his eye. We bullshitted a bit, then he said, "Okay, let's get down to it. What exactly is the nature of your business?"

I told him I wanted to cut a deal to put shows in Chicago Stadium.

"You mean you need to meet with Arthur Wirtz."

"Yeah," I said. "I guess that is what I mean."

"Okay," he said. "I'm going to get up and go the bathroom. And while I'm in the bathroom, you're going to put something in my jacket."

"What am I going to put in your jacket?" I asked.

He told me, and it wasn't two tickets to *The Wiz*.

"Well, I don't have that," I said.

"You have to get it," he said.

"Oh, God."

"Can you have it by lunchtime?" he asked.

"Yeah," I said, "I guess so."

"Good. Come back here at lunchtime, put it in my pocket, and you will have your meeting with Arthur Wirtz."

A few days later, I go to meet Mr. Wirtz. A two o'clock appointment. He had an office in the Furniture Mart, which he owned. I gave my name to the secretary, then sat, waiting. Now and then, I asked the secretary, "How much longer?" and she smiled and said, "Any time now." Her name, as I learned later, was Gertrude Knowles, and she was fantastic, a multimillionaire with a piece of every one of Wirtz's deals. (He could be very generous.) Two o'clock became three o'clock; three o'clock became four o'clock. I was angry. "What's his problem?" I asked Ms. Knowles. "We had an appointment. I got things to do."

"Relax," she said. "He does this to everybody. If you want something from him, you have to wait."

"I am thinking of leaving," I told her.

"Don't worry," she said. "I'll get you in there."

Another thirty minutes went by. I couldn't stand it. I was going wild. I stood up and said, "To hell with this, I'm out of here."

"No, don't," she said, "I'll get you in right now."

She walked over, opened the door, stuck her head inside, and said, "Jerry Weintraub has been out here waiting three hours. It is time for you to see him."

A voice boomed back: "Okay, fine, bring him in."

It was the biggest office I'd ever seen. Everything was covered in brass and wood. Behind him was a credenza filled with Steuben glass. On his desk—it was the size of an aircraft carrier—was a model of the Wirtz family yacht, the *Blackhawk*, and a plane. Mr. Wirtz was alone in this office, and had been all afternoon, this enormous man, signing checks, which were piled beside him. He did not greet me. He just went on signing.

"What do you want?" he asked, without looking up.

That's what he said. After all that sitting and waiting and him being in here all the time by himself, with his checks and signing pen.

"What do I want?" I said. "I'll tell you what I want. Screw you! That's what I want!"

Now he looked up, stunned, as if I had slapped him across the face.

My God, he was huge!

"Excuse me," he asked, "what did you say?"

This man was power, you have to understand that. He was the boss, the man sitting on top of a very tough town. This was Chicago. Sam Giancana was there. Tony the Ant was there. Wirtz was no gangster, of course, but he had the gangsters, and had the police, and had the firemen, and had the aldermen, and had the attorney general, and had the mayor and the governor and everything else.

"You heard me," I told him. "Screw you."

He was more surprised than angry—confused, concerned.

"Why?" he asked. "What's the matter?"

"I've been waiting out there four hours," I said. "Then, I finally get in here, and you don't even look up and say hello, how are you? You don't shake my hand, or offer me a drink of water? What kind of bullshit is that? I'm a human being, you know. I'm standing here."

And he sat back and looked at me—and this looking took longer than it should have—smiled and laughed. He stood up, walked around the desk, sat in the chair next to me, shook my hand, and said, "It is nice to meet you. I am Arthur Wirtz."

And I shook his hand and said, "Nice to meet you. I'm Jerry Weintraub."

We made a deal that very night, negotiating the terms for

hours. At one point, he said, "Hey, Jerry, you look hungry," went into the little kitchen he had off his office and cooked me a steak. This big guy, this big shot, sleeves rolled up, standing over a T-bone. He loved me because I told him to go screw himself. No one had ever done that. We finished the last points at 9:00 P.M.

"Okay," he said, "now I have to get the board of directors to ratify the deal."

I was pissed. "You mean, I stayed here all night negotiating and you can't even do a deal with me? You have to wait for someone else?"

"We don't have to wait," he said. "We'll do it now."

He led me down the hall to an empty boardroom. There was a round table with ornate chairs and leather blotters and beautiful lamps with green shades, each throwing a pool of light. Arthur sat at the head of the table, struck the gavel, then said, "Meeting in session." He read the main points of our contract aloud, asked if any members of the board were opposed, any objections, waited a moment, as if expecting an answer—"Good news," he said to me, "no objections"—announced the contract ratified, then brought down the gavel, adjourning the meeting.

"I did that for a reason," he explained. "I wanted to show you something. You're going to make a lot of money. Do it yourself. Don't ever go public. Be in charge of your own destiny."

It was the beginning of a friendship that lasted decades. We made millions of dollars together. He was my mentor in the world of arenas and concerts and filling seats. He made me a king. He got me exclusive deals in hockey buildings all over the country. The Stadium in Chicago, the Olympia in Detroit, the Garden in New York, the Forum in LA—he controlled them all. We worked as partners, put on shows, filled the seats, paid the band and other expenses, paid our taxes, split the rest. He was supposed to be anti-Semitic. It was a rumor. You heard it whispered, but there was no truth to it. I loved him, and he loved me. We hung out together, vacationed together. Remember the model of the boat on his desk? Well, he gave me use of that boat—the real thing, not the model—whenever I wanted to get away.

Wirtz had a way about him. It was often hard to tell if he was joking. One night, when we had Zeppelin at the Stadium, security confiscated joints and other contraband from the kids as they came in the door. By showtime, the back room was filled with bags of dope and pills. One of the cops asked Wirtz what should be done with the stuff. Arthur thought for a moment, then said, "Well, why can't we sell it back to them as they leave?"

By the late seventies, I had so much going in LA, it left no time for Chicago. I stopped going, stopped hanging out, bullshitting, and instead sent Bill McKenzie, the chief financial officer of my company, to talk to Mr. Wirtz and settle up after a show. The money from the city had come to seem automatic. Then something changed. The profit dipped, the numbers went down. One year I made eighteen million with Arthur, the next year I made fifteen million, then thirteen million.

My accountant called.

"Jerry," he said, "something is wrong in Chicago. The receipts have been going up, but the backend stays the same. I think you're being shorted."

"Shorted?"

"Yeah. Shorted. You're being ripped off."

I called Mr. Wirtz.

"What's happening with the money?" I asked.

"If you want to talk to me," he said, "come to Chicago and talk to me."

I went to his office.

"Okay," he said, "what's the problem?"

I had written all the numbers on a sheet of paper, costs, ticket sales, and where I was coming up thin. He looked these over. "So you think you are being shorted?" he asked.

"Yeah," I said.

"How much you think you've lost?" he asked.

"Well," I said, "I think I'm behind about a million and a half dollars."

"Hold on," he told me, opened his desk drawer, took out a paper, looked at it, then said, "Not bad. You're only off a little. I actually owe you two million."

"What's going on?" I demanded.

"Don't get hot," he said. "I have every penny of it for you right here. You would have had it months ago if you had not been such a bastard and come here and been with me and talked to me and done business with me. You should have been here taking care of your business," he told me. "You weren't taking care of your business. This is a good lesson for you."

Years later, when Mr. Wirtz was dying, I went to Chicago and sat by his hospital bed. He could hardly talk. He was just a mountain of a man under the sheets, with the tubes, and the nurses coming in and out, but he was still sharp and missed nothing. You could see it in his eyes.

Once I was established in the entertainment business, I began to see the possibility of shows everywhere. All life was theater and I wanted to put it on a stage and sell tickets. I wanted to produce everything. This is when Billy Friedkin started calling me "Presents." As in, "Hey, Presents!" "How you doing, Presents?" I wanted to put the world under a marquee that read: "Jerry Weintraub Presents." I began to expand away from concerts, pursuing fantasies of the Great White Way. Like every kid from the boroughs, I dreamed of Broadway. I put on a few small shows but realized that to be good, I would need a teacher and guide. If you want to learn, find a person who knows and study him or her.

Which is how one day in 1968, I found myself in the office of Frank Loesser, that Broadway legend, author of, among others, *Where's Charley?*, *How to Succeed in Business Without Really Trying*, and, my favorite, *Guys and Dolls*. Frank Loesser worked in movies, too—he had been under contract with Universal— but he will always be associated with the theater.

He worked in a big office on 57th Street. There was an upright piano and a view of the city. New York is like an infinite library, with everyone you ever wanted to meet tucked in a little room. Knock on this door, Sinatra answers. Knock on that door, Presley answers. Knock on this door, Frank Loesser answers.

"What the hell can I do for you, kid? Did they send you for the dry cleaning?"

"No, my name is Jerry Weintraub."

"Okay, Jerry Weintraub. What do you want?"

I told him he was my favorite writer in the world, that *Guys and Dolls* was my favorite show, that I was a producer, and was going to produce on Broadway, and told him that he should produce a show with me.

"Why would I do that, kid?"

"Because I'm going to be a great Broadway producer."

Loesser laughed. "All right," he said, "but why not tell me what you are now."

"I told you," I said. "I'm Jerry Weintraub."

He thought a moment, noodled on the piano, notes drifting across the room, then said, "Tell you what. There is a show in London called *Canterbury Tales*." It's in previews. Hot as a pistol. Goddamn, I want to stage that in New York. But so does every other producer on Broadway. You go to London and get me the rights to that show, and we'll produce it together. We'll be partners.

"We got a deal?" he asked.

"Hell, yes, we got a deal."

"And you are again...?"

"Jerry Weintraub."

"Okay, Jerry. Go get it."

Loesser said everything but "fetch."

I had a big career on Broadway later, and owned a stake in several theaters with Jimmy Nederlander, who ran one of the great organizations in the history of the business. His name is up there with the Shuberts. But this is how I started, in that office off Broadway, with Loesser calling for this trick: Go to London and snatch the prize from the jaws of a dozen hungry producers.

When I landed at Heathrow Airport, I went straight to a house in Chelsea, where I met Nevill Coghill and Martin Starkie, who produced and adapted the original production of this play, *Canterbury Tales*. I say "this play" because I did not know anything about it. I had heard of Chaucer but did not really know who he was. Maybe if instead of the Air Force I had gone to college...but, as I said, I did go, only my professors were Colonel Tom and Frank Sinatra, who offered neither a core curriculum nor lectures in medieval English poetry. My classes, which were various, included deportment ("Talking Straight With a Buzz On"), History ("The Rise and Fall of Dukes and Kings"), Business ("Don't Be a Sucker"), vocations ("Knowing What You Got, and Using It"), and philosophy ("I think therefore I dance").

I knocked on the door of the house. A beautiful-looking guy came out in tight white pants with no shirt. He was Coghill and Starkie's butler. His name was Bunky. He led me to a dining room, where lunch had been set out. The producers were waiting, proper, English, amused. Referring back to my class with Professor Sinatra ("Knowing What You Got, and Using It"), and considering myself a not terrible-looking kid, I switched gears, turned a little flirty. We talked about the play. As I said, I did not know who Chaucer was, but the show had been a hit in previews and Loesser said get it, so here I was, drinking Perrier and asking the guys to pass the dill. I could not have the show, they said. Not yet, anyway. They were still making up their mind, had to meet with everyone, and so forth. But I persisted. I went over there every day for a week, pitching, selling. We got to be friends. They invited me to go with them to the opening night, which was a real honor.

We got to the theater. Freyer, Carr, Harris, Merrick, Bloomgarden—all the Broadway big shots were there, looking to acquire rights to the show. They were craning in their seats, looking over, perplexed, trying to figure, *Who is the kid with Coghill and Starkie? Is that Jerry Weintraub? Doesn't he work with Elvis? What the hell is he doing here?* The lights go down, the curtain comes up on a road in the country, a cart filled with travelers, each itching to tell his or her tale. The crowd is silent, rapt, but I'm not hearing it, not seeing it. I'm thinking about

Frank Loesser: "Go to London, get the rights, we'll produce it together. We'll be partners." I'm with these guys, have them to myself…but the show will end, the party will start, the drinks and congratulations and Broadway hotshots, and I will miss my chance.

I have to act now!

I leaned over and whispered to Starkie—we're in tuxedos—"I'm sorry, Martin, and don't want to alarm you, but a pain is shooting up my left arm and into my chest."

Starkie looks over, thinks a moment, takes my wrist and says, "We're getting out of here right away. We're going to the hospital."

"No," I whispered. "I can't take you out of your opening night."

"To hell with opening night," said Starkie. "You're sick!"

Starkie and Coghill led me out of the seat and rushed me up the aisle, the whispers trailing us, out the door. I was slumped in back of the car. Martin was feeling my head, taking my pulse. We go by the Hilton. "Look," I said, "if I can just get in there, sit down, have a glass of water, maybe I'll feel better."

We found a couch in the lobby. These guys were all over me, pale with fear, certain I was going to die.

"How do you feel?" asked Coghill.

"A little better," I said.

"What can we do for you?" asked Starkie.

"Well," I said, "I really want to buy the show."

"Will that make you feel better?" asked Coghill.

"Oh, Nevill," said Starkie, "just sell him the goddamn show."

I bought it for ten grand. (My check bounced, but that's another story.) With the terms agreed on, my condition improved greatly. The play was over by then. We went to the cast party.

Everyone was there. Coghill stood on a chair and made the announcement. "The American rights to *Canterbury Tales* have been sold to Jerry Weintraub." All those Broadway producers stood dumbstruck, couldn't figure it out. Neither could Loesser. He kept saying "How, Jerry, how?"

I'm not saying you should fake a heart attack every time, only in a pinch.

As I said, in those years, I wanted to acquire, perfect, produce, and sell tickets to everything that moved me. It was not just about money. It was about love. I wanted to share whatever electrified me. In 1976, I was, for example, mesmerized by Dorothy Hamill, the perky, young, short-haired figure skater dominating the Winter Olympics. She won the gold medal, but it was her charm and style that made her a sensation. I was glued to my television. I did not want to miss a minute of it.

One afternoon, I was talking to Roone Arledge, who was producing the Olympics for ABC. I said, "Look, Roone, if you happen to talk to Dorothy Hamill, ask if she needs someone to advise her. This all happened so fast. She must be overwhelmed."

Ten minutes later—*boom!*—the phone rings. It's Dorothy. She asks to meet right after the closing ceremonies. The whole world wants her, and she does not know what to do. We met in the lobby of a hotel in Providence, Rhode Island. We talked for hours. She had a difficult family situation. She was eighteen, and, like most of the kids who skate—because they practice twenty-four hours, seven days a week—she had not had much interaction with the outside world. She was very childlike. The only people she knew had either staked their careers on her success, or staked their careers on someone other than her being successful. She asked me to manage her, take care of her, and so forth. I made several moves right from the hotel lobby. I called the guys that ran Bristol-Myers, for example, and made a deal for a shampoo called Short N' Sassy. Because that was Dorothy. I called ABC and made a deal for eight Dorothy Hamill TV specials. Within a few hours, this girl who had never seen a nickel in all her life was a multimillionaire. It was fantastic. She came to California after that and lived with me and Jane. My friends were her friends, and she married Dean Martin's son, Dino Jr.

The Grand Master

Okay, here's my favorite of the crazy, why-the-hell-not-try-it stories of those years. In the summer of 1972, I got hooked on the World Championship of Chess, which was being shown on PBS and *ABC Wide World of Sports*, with Bobby Fischer, the American, playing Boris Spassky, the Russian, in Reykjavik, Iceland. The men crouched over the chessboard in utter silence for hours on end. I do not know a thing about chess, have never played it and don't want to—I was relying on the PBS commentator, who moved pieces around a board to explain the game—but I was transfixed by Fischer. He was tall, with blue eyes and wild hair and the slow, graceful motions of a hypnotist or magician. He sat stone still, radiating a weird charisma. It came right through the set. I rushed home every night to have dinner in front of the TV. You could not get me out of the house. I was mesmerized.

Jane finally confronted me.

"What is wrong with you?" she asked. "Have you gone nuts?"

"What are you talking about?" I said.

"You. You sit in front of the TV for hours every night,

watching a chess match. You don't know anything about chess, not even the rules."

"I'm not watching a chess match," I told her. "I'm watching this guy Bobby Fischer."

"Why?"

"Because he's a star."

"You're insane."

"Oh, really," I said. "I will show you how insane I am."

I picked up the phone and called Icelandic Airways. I asked when they would next fly to Reykjavik.

Nine o'clock tonight.

"Good," I said. "I want a seat."

I got on a plane to Reykjavik. There was a young guy in the next seat. We started talking. He was a priest and also a grand master at chess. He knew everyone in that world, and had actually played Fischer and Spassky. He asked why I was going to Iceland. I told him I was going to meet Bobby Fischer.

"You're going to meet Bobby Fischer?" he said, surprised. "Do you have an appointment with him?"

"No," I said. "I'm just going to track him down."

"Oh, no," he said. "You can't just track down Bobby Fischer. He doesn't talk to anyone, doesn't go anywhere. He is locked off from the world."

"What? Why?"

"Because he's crazy."

It was the first indication that the goal I had set for myself—get in touch with Fischer, talk to him, pitch him, sign him, make him rich, and take a percentage—would be more difficult to achieve than I had thought.

I reserved a room in the hotel where most of the chess people were staying. The lobby was filled with tables, each with a chessboard, where grand masters were locked in combat. After each move, they hit a button to freeze the clock. *Click. Click. Click.* It made a kind of rhythm. A group of reporters, mostly Americans, were taking notes in the corner, searching for a new angle on the story. Spassky wouldn't talk to them because the KGB had forbidden it. Fischer wouldn't talk to them because he was nuts. When I went to the desk to check in, one of the reporters recognized me. He came over with a microphone; I was just off the plane, burned out and groggy, and now I was on the radio.

"Are you Jerry Weintraub?" he asked.

"Yeah," I said.

"You represent rock acts, Elvis Presley, John Denver. What are you doing in Reykjavik?"

"I'm here to see Bobby Fischer."

"Do you have an appointment to see Mr. Fischer?"

"No, I don't have an appointment. I don't even know him."

"Then how are you going to see him? He won't see anybody."

"Don't worry," I said. "I'll see him."

"Do you play chess?" the reporter asked. "Are you a chess fanatic?"

"I don't even know how to play chess," I told him. "I don't know anything about it."

"Then why are you here?"

"I'm here because I've been watching Bobby Fischer on TV," I said. "I am glued to the set every night. He's like Mick Jagger. He's like Elvis. The man is a rock star."

I got my key and went to my room—it was the only hotel in Iceland, the rooms were little white cubes—climbed into bed, and passed out. A long, dreamless, time-zone-crossing sleep. The phone rang. I had the receiver to my ear before I had woken up.

Where the hell am I, half asleep in this tiny white square?

"Yeah?"

"Is this Jerry Weintraub?"

The voice was a spooky, otherworldly whisper.

"Yeah, who is this?"

"Do you really think I'm like Elvis Presley and Mick Jagger?"

"How do you know I said that?"

"I heard you on the radio."

He paused, then said, "We need to meet."

"Great," I said. "Where, when?"

I was whispering, too, acting as if someone were listening, as if the CIA had bugged the phones.

"Come to the sixth floor," he said, "take the steps, stand by the door. I will be waiting for you."

I scuttled down the stairs like a crab. (*Am I being followed?*) When I crossed the landing and stepped through the door, I was standing next to Bobby Fischer. The whole world was trying to talk to this genius recluse, this Howard Hughes. I mean, legions of reporters were camped in the lobby with this one goal in mind, and here I was, having pulled it off without trying, in less than a day. (*What can I say? The Lord takes care of me.*) Fischer motioned me to follow him. He took me down the hall to his room. It was disgusting. There were half-eaten cheeseburgers, old pizzas, boxes of shit, Coke cans, crap lying everywhere. And the smell! My God, the smell. Here and there, on the floor, on the bed, *Playboy* magazines were opened, and I am sure he'd been masturbating all over the centerfolds. Fischer was standing in the middle of all this, with an air of "Look what time hath wrought."

"I have no money," he whispered.

"What do you mean, you have no money?"

"The Chess Federation won't give me any money," he said. "I have nothing."

"No problem," I said. "We'll get you some money."

He looked at me. His eyes were intelligent and calculating, but their setting (his narrow, ascetic face, the face of a mystic or monk) was not reassuring.

"You can get me money?" he asked.

"Of course I can get you money," I told him.

"Good," he said. "I want to go bowling."

"Then go bowling," I said.

"I can't afford it," he said. "I have no money."

"I'll figure it out," I said. "By tomorrow, there will be a deal for you."

"Then can we go bowling?"

"Yes," I said. "Then we can go bowling."

He asked me to go with him to the match. So the next night, when Fischer climbed out of his car, with the journalists clamoring for a quote, I was the corner man at his side. I sat behind him as he played. A few days before, I had been watching this scene on television. Now here I was, in the background of the establishing shot. I had gone inside the screen. I played off Fischer, reacted to his every move.

I looked annoyed when he looked annoyed. I looked amused when he looked amused. We drove back to the hotel, huddled together in confab.

Then I took him bowling.

"How are we going to make money?" he asked.

"I've been thinking about that," I told him. "And I have a great idea. I'm going to call my friends in LA. You're going to make a record."

He looked at me like I was nuts. Being looked at like you're crazy by a crazy man is a singular experience. "What do you mean a record?" he asked. "I can't even carry a tune."

"No, you're not going to sing," I told him. "You're going to teach."

"Teach what?"

"The record is going to be Bobby Fischer teaching a six-year-old kid, who knows nothing about chess, how to play. And the cover will be a chess board. And with it, we will include chess pieces in a plastic bag. We'll sell it at Christmas. It will be huge."

I called Warner Music the next day. I sold the deal over the phone, just like that. First of all, the record executives loved the idea of getting a phone call from Reykjavik. They loved the idea of being in business with Fischer, too. He was the mystery man of the moment, a mercurial genius, all over television but nowhere at all. What's more, it was a great idea. The label gave us a lot of money for it. I don't remember the figure, but it was a primary number followed by many zeros. The contract came, Fischer signed it. Then I had another idea, which appeared to me in a vision: Boris Spassky and Bobby Fischer playing a winner-take-all match in a glass box on a casino floor in Las Vegas. Could you imagine the scene, the bookmakers and high rollers and celebrities? We would sell it as a heavyweight title fight, the World Championship of Chess. For a minute, I even thought it would happen. I did not yet understand Fischer, and how nutty he was.

He flipped out in Reykjavik a few nights later. This was in

the arena in the middle of a match. He was sitting there, head in his palm, drumming his fingers on his cranium. Every few seconds, he looked at the ceiling and shuddered. He leaped to his feet as if he'd been burned and ran across the floor. He went through the crowd as if he were being chased. Then he was gone, the match forfeited. There was a moment of silence, then you heard his voice, a guttural shout with a hint of Brooklyn, calling, "Jerry Weintraub! Come on, Jerry Weintraub, we're getting out of here."

I followed him into the backseat of the car. We started to drive. "What the hell just happened?" I asked.

"Did you hear it?" he said. "Tell me the truth, did you hear it?"

"Hear what?"

"The whirring, the whirring."

Then he put his fingers to his temples, as if he was holding the dark matter of his brain from spilling across the backseat, and yelled, "I CAN'T THINK!"

When we got back to the hotel, I made some calls, asked around. At first, I did not believe him. He was really crazy, but, you know, he was right—there was whirring in the ceiling. It was the ABC camera, filming for *Wide World of Sports*. Fischer said he could not play until it was taken out, removed.

"No more whirring. No more whirring. No more whirring."

I spoke to Roone Arledge, tried to work something out. Then I came back to Bobby, and said, "Look, Bobby, if you got paid, if there was money on the table, do you think the whirring might go away?"

He stopped pacing and looked at me. At such times, the nuttiness and confusion went out of his eyes, and, for a moment, he was sober and shrewd.

"Sure," he said, "it might go away."

"Okay," I said, "let me see what I can do."

I spoke to producers at ABC, gave them the rundown, then came back to Fischer with twenty-five thousand dollars. After that, he did not hear the whirring. He won the tournament, but the incident was a prelude, a glimpse into his soul, which was a morass, brilliance knotted with neurosis, paranoia, and fear. The guy was really something.

He moved to LA. He was brilliant at chess, but lost in the world. He bailed out of the record deal and everything else. He did not trust the businessmen, he did not trust me, he did not trust anyone. There were voices in his head. He wandered, tortured by the whirring of imaginary machines. He let himself go, typical crazy man stuff. He was a target for charismatics, a question mark in search of an easy answer. He got hooked up with a cult in the Valley, the Assembly Church of God. He fell under the sway of a high-ranking member, Dr. Stanley Rader, a total con man. Rader was an accountant from New York who had seen the light. He had been Jewish before he was baptized into the sect—in a bathtub in the Mandarin Hotel in Hong Kong—by the church's founder, Herbert Armstrong. This is the craziness Fischer fell into after Iceland. In this way, everything we planned, everything he could have been and done, went away. He ended up living in the basement of the church and became utterly, totally, and completely insane.

The Death of the King

E lvis is dead."
    I was in Malibu, the morning of August 16, 1977,
when the call came. It was Roone Arledge, who had just become
the head of ABC News. His people had picked up the 911 call
on a police scanner. "What are you talking about?" I asked.

"We just got the news," he said. "Elvis Presley is dead."

I was supposed to meet Elvis in Portland, Maine, the next
day. We were going on tour. He had been at home, in Graceland, getting in shape for the road. He had played racquetball
on his private court, sat at his piano, sung "Unchained Melody,"
gone upstairs, and died—they found him several hours later on
the floor of his bathroom.

My second line rang. It was Joe Esposito, Elvis's right hand.
He was calling from the bathroom in Graceland. He was stand-
ing next to Elvis's body, waiting for the police to arrive. He said,
"Jerry, we need you here right away."

I got the next plane to Memphis. I stared out the window. The
sun hung over the clouds like a fiery eye. Celebrity—that's what
killed Elvis. Fame had shut him out of the world. He couldn't go
to dinner. He couldn't take his kid to the park. He was always

inside. He went to bed at 3:00 A.M. and woke up at noon. His life was abnormal. He dressed different and looked different. He was the first real rock star, a freak in this regard. There was no one like him. Sinatra had New York, Los Angeles, Chicago. Presley had all that plus Lafayette, Louisiana, and Knoxville, Tennessee. He could draw a hundred thousand people to a field in Macon, Georgia. His stardom was unprecedented. It isolated him until his isolation became intolerable. The very talent that connected him to millions kept him sequestered. Yes, he had friends, the Memphis mafia, guys he grew up with, but it wasn't enough. He treated his condition with drugs. When you're a celebrity, if you want a pill, you will have it. He was really a tragic figure.

I took a car to Graceland. What a scene. The news had hit the streets before it was broadcast. People poured out of houses and stood on the grass median strips with tears streaming down their faces. The city was mourning. My car slowed as it approached the mansion. Thousands of people had gathered in front of the gates, their faces reflecting the strobe of police lights. I saw children waving American flags, babies held aloft by mothers, Teamsters weeping without shame, hawkers selling T-shirts and locks of hair. I went into the house, a simple suburban home that Elvis had done up. The Stamps Quartet was singing in the living room, shouting and praising the Lord. Gospel was the soundtrack of the day. The house was packed with hangers-on and celebrities. I saw Ann-Margret, in a bodysuit, her face streaked with mascara. I saw the preacher Rex Humbard waving his arms and talking about the short-term occupancy of man, who rents on this earth and does not own.

Thinking back, I realize I've probably combined a few days in my mind, but it was an irrational moment, a whirlwind, a picture drawn by a kid who cannot stay within the lines.

I looked in the coffin. There was Elvis, done up in his finery, his hair slicked back and his face just as white as porcelain. He was a saint now, a martyr to the pop gods, headed straight for the seventh heaven.

Someone tapped me on the shoulder, whispered in my ear: "Vernon and Colonel Tom are in the back. They want to see you right away." Vernon was Elvis's father. I went through the kitchen into the maid's room, where the men were huddled. The bed was covered with telegrams, thousands of condolences that had been pouring in—from the queen of England, from the president of the United States, from the most important people in the world. The men were arguing—well, if not arguing, then having a heated discussion about whether it was appropriate to sell souvenirs to the mourners in the street. Hawkers were already out there pushing memorabilia, and the attitude was, well, why should we let them take our money? I got between them and said something like, "What's wrong with you guys? The body's in the next room. We're about to leave for the funeral. Have some respect." I'm not putting them down. I think they were in shock, had not quite realized what happened, that Elvis was never coming back. What a bizarre moment, the entire world gathered around this house in tears, and, in a room in the house, the old man and the Colonel arguing about T-shirts.

We went to the funeral in a long line of white Cadillacs. These had been brought from all over the South for the occasion. I was in the car behind the hearse. Now and then, when I see newsreels shot that day, I know I am in that second Cadillac. The ride was unbelievable. It was as if the president had died. The streets were lined with people, black people and white people and children and babies. In a crazy way, it was very much the ideal of America, what our country should be about. When I had been in the South as a kid, it was segregated. I told you. On the white side, we were shooed away like rats. On the black side, we were given plates piled with food. Of course, I did not understand the meaning of that, all the oppression and suffering and misery that implied. But riding in that car in Memphis, I saw a new America. There was no hatred, no segregation, no bigotry. None of that shit. Everyone in the crowd was connected by a shared love and a shared grief. The death of Elvis marked the end of an era, but it also marked the birth of something new.

Making Movies

I n 1974, George Bush, who was U.S. ambassador to the United Nations, asked me to help him throw a party for his fellow ambassadors from around the globe. The party started with a concert by John Denver in Carnegie Hall. It was good for Bush, but it was also good for John, singing for all these men and women who would go back to their countries and talk him up, and maybe even invite him to perform. It's a twofer. In helping George Bush, I was helping John Denver, and in helping John Denver, I was helping Jerry Weintraub.

The show was followed by a party in the apartment I owned on West Fifty-fourth Street in Manhattan. All the New York big shots were there. Jane had helped me put together the list. At some point, after the second cocktail, say, she brought the director Robert Altman over to meet me. Altman had already directed some of his greatest films, *M*A*S*H*, *Brewster McCloud*, *McCabe and Mrs. Miller*. He had a reputation for being difficult, a brilliant pain in the ass. He did not like producers, studio executives, money men, or anyone who tried to tell him what to do. He was given *M*A*S*H*—the movie that made his name—only after it had been turned down by a half dozen other directors.

The room was packed with ambassadors and dignitaries, but when we talked, it was just him and me. We connected right away. He asked if I had ever produced films. I told him I had not. "Well, you should consider it," he said. "You would make a great producer. You have just the right personality."

"What kind of personality does it take?"

I was trying to figure out if I was being complimented or put down.

"It's temperament," he told me. "Smarts and all that, but also the ability to sell an idea, attract talent to that idea, bring out the best in the players, while, at the same time keeping everything in line. If you can talk to people, get them to do things because they think it's their own idea, you will be a great producer."

He talked a little more, then said, "You know, I have a script, it's gonna be a great movie, it's in a drawer at home, maybe you want to take a look at it. Maybe you'll want to produce it."

The script came by messenger the next day. *Nashville*, by Joan Tewkesbury. I sit. I read. And the more I read, the less I get it as a movie. There are a million characters spinning through a million plots. I don't get it. I call Altman, set a meeting. We go to a restaurant in LA. "Look, I'm going to be very honest with you," I told him. "I do not understand it. I was totally lost. But I want to produce it."

"You don't get it, but you want to produce it?"

"Yeah."

"Why?"

"Because you get it, and I get you."

Here's the lesson: Know what you're buying. Was I buying *Nashville*? No, I was buying Robert Altman. I did not understand the script, but Altman did, and it was Altman who was going to make the movie. This is the dynamic you see when you read in the newspaper that a corporation has overpaid for a tiny upstart. You scratch your head and wonder: why? Well, maybe it's not the company that they are buying but an executive who works at the company, or a patent, or an idea still in the pipeline. I did not understand the script, but I was totally sold on the director.

Altman then explained the movie to me, each scene and beat, how the things I had seen in the script would be brought to life, how all the strands would converge in a rush at the end. I walked out of there convinced I had made the right deal.

Altman had not told me he had already shopped the script all over town, had pitched to and been turned away from every major studio. When I showed up, many of the executives seemed pained. The fact is, these guys had been asking me to work with them for years. Because they had seen me work with Presley, because they had seen me work with Sinatra, because they thought I could perform. Now, when I finally showed up, it was with a script they had already rejected and a director, who, while being a genius, was considered a giant pain in the ass.

Here's what they would say: "Jeez, Jerry, we would love to work with you, as you know, love to have you in the business, but this is just not the right project. If it were anything else, blah, blah, blah."

After I had been all over town, I went back to Altman and said, "Look, I can't get the money, I can't sell it, so here's what I decided: I am going to put my own money into it, a million-nine, just to get us going."

Altman looked horrified. "No, Jerry. Don't put up your own money. That's not how it works. You get them to put up their money."

"We're beyond that," I told him. "We're into the contingencies here."

"Well, it makes me feel funny," he said.

He probably did not want someone with money in the picture so close to him—it's a comfort to think of the money people, those who lose if you fail, as a far-off "them," the boys in suits.

"It's just how we're going to get it going," I said. "We'll figure the rest of it on the fly."

I'll tell you my biggest talent. When I believe in something, it's going to get done. When people say, "No," I don't hear it. When people say, "That's a bad idea," I don't believe them. When people say, "It won't happen," I pretend they're joking.

In the case of *Nashville*, everything worked out very well and very quickly. Soon after I fronted the money, I sold the TV rights to one of the networks. This was unheard of, selling broadcast rights before the film has been made, but as I told Altman, we were in the world of contingencies.

Marty Starger, who ran ABC Entertainment, and Leonard Goldenson, president of ABC—they made it happen. Goldenson, who started the network, had been in the movie business for years. When I told him about *Nashville*, he said, "I want in on that." He put up the money—recouping my investment— then brought Paramount in as the distributor. Paramount was being run by Frank Yablans and Robert Evans. By the time the movie was released, Barry Diller and Michael Eisner, who had worked with me at ABC, and become great friends of mine, had taken over.

Well, you probably know the rest. *Nashville* was a phenomenon, one of those projects that launches a career, the low-budget long-shot that turns into a masterpiece. Pauline Kael called it a new *Citizen Kane* in the *New Yorker*. That was my first review, my debut in the business. Everything I did later was built on the success of *Nashville*, from saying yes when everyone else said no. The experience taught an important lesson: Work with the best people. If you have the best writers, the best actors, and the best director and fail, okay, fine, there is even something noble in it; but if you fail with garbage, then you are left with nothing to hang your spirits on.

Besides, life is too short to be spent in the company of morons.

It was an amazing time for me. In those years, I haunted the Arts and Leisure section of the *New York Times*. The first page of the section was, say, Theater. You open it up, I had a play. You turn the page, I had a movie. Turn it again, I had an album. Next page, I had a TV special. All at the same time. That's when I knew I was really making it, when I opened the Arts pages of the *Times* and was represented as a presents or a producer in every part of the section. And it was not a one-time thing. It happened a number of times. I mean, if something is fun, if you like it, well, you would like to like it again and again.

In those years, things just sort of happened. Around this time, I bought this stunningly beautiful Rolls-Royce limo, and a hired driver. No one else had a car like that. It popped. One day, I had a meeting at CBS with Clive Davis. My car was parked in front. It started to rain. William Paley, who owned CBS and was one of the legendary power media guys—he could make or break careers—came down in the elevator, stepped outside, and couldn't get a car. You know how it is in New York when the rain is coming down. So one of Paley's guys spotted my car and said, "Hey, that's Jerry Weintraub's Rolls. He's upstairs in a meeting. Take it. It will drop you off and be back before Jerry is finished."

Paley said, "I can't take someone else's car."

"Don't be silly. Jerry would want you to take it. He would he honored."

So they convinced Paley, then convinced my driver, who at first objected—*No, I work for Mr. Weintraub*—then was talked into it. He dropped off Paley and was waiting for me when I got out.

On the way to my apartment, he said, "You know, Mr. Weintraub, when you were upstairs, I took another man home in the car."

Like he was confessing an infidelity, a love affair.

"You can't do that," I said. "You're my driver."

"I know, I told them, but they insisted," said the driver. "The guy was some big deal."

"Who was it?"

He had no idea.

The next day, I was sitting in my office, and my secretary rang in. William Paley was calling.

No. I couldn't believe it.

I picked up.

"Yes, Mr. Paley?"

"Are you Jerry Weintraub?"

"Yes."

"Well, Mr. Weintraub, I want to thank you for use of your car yesterday. Very generous of you."

"Oh, sure, no problem, don't mention it."

He asked me to come to his office so he could thank me in person. I went over, we sat, hit it off. He asked why I wasn't producing for television. I said something like, "Well, because no one asked." He called in two of his key guys and said, "Give Jerry a couple of our summer slots. He's going to put together some shows for us." See how life works? A low-pressure system looms over the Atlantic, and I wind up making TV shows for CBS.

Every ten years, I have built a new career without quite meaning to or even knowing it. (The pattern is apparent only when I look back.) I had already been an agent, a promoter, a manager, and a creator of shows. I now became a film producer. God, it was fun. The movies had always loomed large in my imagination—and now I was part of that world. I remember the early days, when I would drive onto the studio lots to meet executives and pitch my ideas. It was exactly like what Hollywood should be. There were crowds of extras dressed as cowboys, conquistadors, whatever, rushing set to set, shouting, alive. It was like being a kid again, reliving the thrill of driving into movie land. Just because you get older, make money and lose money, does not mean you should forget how exciting it all is.

This was the midseventies. It was an interregnum, a moment between eras. The new Hollywood of auteurs and independent producers was just coming into view, while the old Hollywood of bosses was just fading away. Most of the studio heads today are not bosses in that classic sense. They do not own the studios. They work for a board of directors and can be fired in five minutes. The old moguls, the guys who came from the garment trade, worked only for themselves. They owned the industry as you might own a house or a car. It was theirs. Harry Cohn. Joseph Schenk. Louis B. Mayer. Jack Warner. These men have since been vilified and condemned by the people who replaced them—that's what always happens—but they were in fact terrific pioneers. There is a lot to be learned from their sense of ownership and pride, and how they took responsibility for everything, from the first draft to the final cut.

Soon after I got into the business, Lew Wasserman asked me to come work for him at MCA. "Jerry, we're friends, we go back," he said. "It's only right that you should make pictures with us."

"I already have a deal," I told him. "It's a big deal. You don't want my deal."

"Don't tell me what I want," he said.

"Okay, you want to make a deal? Fine. Good. Bring your lawyer over to my house and we'll make a deal."

I went back to MCA with Lenny Goldberg, my partner in those years. It was coming full circle. I started as an assistant at MCA and returned with the big contract. My first day, I went to eat at the commissary. I was sitting with my corned beef and cream soda, and here came Lew, smiling. He sat at my table. He said, "Jerry, I can't tell you how happy it makes me that you're back." We talked about this and that, then, as he got up, he turned and said, "Oh, and Jerry. Do me one favor. Stay off the WATS line!"

Family

The seventies were crazy everywhere, but crazier in Los
Angeles. It was the era of freewheeling drugs and sex,
the rag end of the sixties. I refer to sprees, to strange couplings
and triplings, to nights that started with beer and wine and
ended with cocaine and capsules, to debaucheries too various
to chronicle. In a sense, we were all Robert Mitchum, smoking
rope in bed with two girls while the sun was still noon high. We
thought it was normal. You would walk into a house for a pool
party, and there, on the cocktail table in the center of the living
room, as if it were nuts or cooked shrimp, would be a platter of
cocaine. We did it because we were stupid, because we did not
know the danger.

When I talk about my drug years, I am talking about
twenty-four months in the middle of the seventies. I was in the
rock and roll world, which meant I was around the stuff all the
time. Of course, it was more than mere proximity. I was fun
when I was high, talkative and all-encompassing. I could go forever, never be done talking. To some extent, I was really self-
medicating, using the drugs to skate over issues in my own life.
The fact is, money and success had come so fast, while I was

away doing something else, not paying attention, that, when I finally realized where I was and just what I had, I could not understand it. There was this voice in my head, saying, *Who do you think you are? What do you think you did? You are a fraud! You don't deserve any of this!*

I tortured myself, and let the anxiety well up, then beat back the anxiety with the drugs, on and on, until one day, I stood up and said, "Screw it. That's over. I'm done."

No rehab, no counseling, nothing like that. Just a moment of clarity, in which I saw myself from the outside, the mess I was making, the waste. I was slipping, not working as hard as I used to. I started leaving the office early on Fridays, then skipping Fridays altogether. Then I started leaving early on Thursdays, then arriving late on Mondays. I was letting myself go. Then one day, I just decided, *It has to stop.* I threw away the pills and bottles, took a cold shower, had a barbershop shave, and stepped into the cool of Sunset Boulevard, and began fresh.

Maybe it had to do with my family situation. I was a father again. I already had my son, Michael, but Jane wanted a baby. As we could not have a child of our own, for reasons I won't go into, we decided to adopt. By this time, Jane's career had taken a backseat to my own. It seems as if she planned it this way all along, though she calls it a natural progression. Jane brought me to LA, introduced me to the key people, made her world my world, set me up, mentored and loved me. Then, when my career took off, she let herself drift from the public eye, did fewer shows, made fewer records, and so forth, and not because she was forced to—there were plenty of offers and opportunities. Though she was, in fact, as beautiful and talented and in demand as she had ever been, she was simply tired of that life.

She had become a star at such a young age, had been famous for so long, that she was over it. She wanted another life. She wanted to be a mother.

We pursued a standard adoption, wrote letters, filled out forms. We did not care if it was a boy or a girl. We just wanted a baby. It was many months before we found her in Florida. We learned all about the birth mother, her background, her history, her due date. We tracked it so carefully it felt, at times, as if Jane herself were expecting. Then, when the mother was about seven months pregnant, we got a phone call in the middle of the night—it's over, you will not be getting the baby. It's impossible to explain how hard this hit us. It felt as if there had been a miscarriage, as if we had lost the baby. It was terrible. Jane went into a deep funk. I remember going to see the lawyers and losing it, throwing a stack of papers in the air and shouting, "You bastards, you can't do this to a person! You're killing Jane."

Then, late one night, while we were sitting in the house, moping, wondering what to do next, the phone rang. It was the lawyer. Something had changed. We had the baby. Incredible. She was three days old and would arrive by plane in the morning. I called the manager of Saks Fifth Avenue. He opened the store for us in the middle of the night. (I must have promised him something.) I remember wandering the empty rooms, filling a basket with tiny clothes, Beverly Hills bathed in moonlight out the windows.

We went to LAX at 7.00 A.M. My doctor insisted on coming with us. He wanted to examine the baby before we took possession, "Just to make sure she's healthy, Jerry."

"There really is no point," I told him. "I'm taking this baby no matter what. This is my baby."

"Just hang back," he said. "I don't want you near that baby till I've had a look."

A nurse came off the plane with the bundle. I took the baby from her before the doctor could get close. As I reached for the baby—this was Julie, my oldest daughter, who is wonderful, beautiful, and now thirty-five—my back went out, which is one of the reasons I remember the day so vividly. (My life can be divided into segments: days when I am standing straight, and days when my back has gone out.) The doctor hurried over. "Come on," he said. "Let me just have a look before you go home with that baby."

"This is my baby," I told him.

"Fine," he said, "let me look at your baby."

Luckily, the baby had ten fingers and ten toes and was perfect in every other respect, as I was keeping her no matter what the doctor had to say.

Then we went home. Jane was happy, and I was happy. It was a good time.

A few years later, Jane decided she wanted another baby.

I was against this at first. Not because I did not want another baby, but because I did not want to go through that again, the lawyers and papers and chance of losing the kid at the end, reliving the tumult and heartbreak.

"I'm sorry," I told Jane. "I just can't do it."

Around this time, I hosted a fund-raiser in Las Vegas for the Catholic Charities of Nevada. This was in honor of Frank Sinatra's mother, who, not long before, had been killed in a plane crash while traveling to see Frank perform. A dozen top artists sang at this benefit, including Sinatra himself. There must have been a thousand people in the room. I was seated with an innocuous little guy named Tom Miller, the director of the charities. We started talking.

He said, "I understand you have an adopted child."

"That's true," I told him.

"How old is your child?" he asked.

"She's going to be two," I said.

"Wouldn't you like to adopt another child?" he asked.

"Yes, I would," I said, "but it's impossible to adopt children."

"It's not impossible," he said. "And to prove it's not impossible, I am going to get you a child."

"What are you talking about?"

"I'm talking about the fact that I am going to get you a child," he said.

"How are you going to do that?" I asked.

"Well," he said, "we have the Nevada Catholic Welfare Act and we have a home for unwed mothers. We have a wonderful sister there. I am going to talk to her, and she is going to get the baby that God means for you to have."

"But I'm not a Catholic," I told him.

"I didn't ask about your religion," he said. "I asked if you wanted to have another child."

"Well, yes," I said. "I do."

A week later, the sister visited me and Jane in Beverly Hills. I can still see the two of them walking through the house, from the living room to the baby's room, with the sun going down. We sat in the kitchen. "I have your child," the sister told me. "She is already in the home, she is three months old, and she looks exactly like you."

This was Jamie, who is now thirty-two. She came in a bundle, like something in a storybook. And she did look like me. This experience—the death of Frank's mother, the charity event, the innocuous little man, the nun walking through our house, the baby that looked like me—touched me deeply.

I went to Vegas to see the house where the unwed mothers lived while they were pregnant and the babies stayed until homes could be found. I became involved after the visit and gave a lot of money to help the sisters build a new, better home.

Then my third daughter came. This was not something we planned on. It just happened. One day, the sister called. She said, "Jerry, your new baby has been born."

"My baby, Sister? Come on!"

"Yes, your baby," she said. "She is the most beautiful little girl, with a full head of hair—she is supposed to go to you. Don't you want another child?"

"Of course, I want another child."

Paul Anka was singing in Vegas at the time. He was a client and is still a friend. He had his plane there. He flew her back to Los Angeles. This is Jody, who is just about to turn thirty.

I stayed involved with the charities. I gave money, but, more important, I helped babies find homes and couples find babies. (I am the man to go to when you want what money can't buy.) Friends who wanted to adopt came to me. I consulted and advised, then put them together with the sister, who wandered the mansions of Malibu and Beverly Hills, searching for the heavenly connection, just the right baby for just the right parents. I was part of at least fifty adoptions. I still get calls and letters from my many dozens of godchildren, the scions of powerful Hollywood families. After about twenty years, though, I quit my role as facilitator. I cared too much, and felt burdened by the responsibility—a marriage that ended in divorce, parents who seemed cavalier or abusive. I had taken on more than I could handle. I remain involved with the charities, however, give and do what I can. My family was built in a way unlike the way my mother and father built our family in the Bronx, but it sits on the same bedrock: love and loyalty and concern tempered with a large dose of comedy.

Which brings me to a question I ask myself every day: What kind of a father have I been? Have I been good? Have I helped more than I have hurt? Have I given as much as I have taken? In truth, my children have, at times, had trouble. With depression, with drugs, with all those exotic things that befall kids nowadays. Though I do not like all the things they have done, I am here for them when they are in jeopardy and I do whatever I can when they need help. I sometimes wonder if the root of the problem is in our very circumstances, if the life we have given our children—the money and the cars and the vacations and the private planes—has spoiled the everyday world for them.

Can the child of a rich man have the same ambition as a kid from the Bronx?

One evening, one of my daughters, having just flown on a commercial plane for the first time in her life, called me in a panic. "My God," she said, "the way they jam you in, and make you sit there, in one seat, it's like a prison!"

In the end, though, I think your outlook has less to do with money than with the values your parents exhibit and your own nature. In this, I've been neither perfect nor blameless. I love my children and I think I have been a good father, but there were times when I chose my career over the life of the house. Was I there for every recital, or play, or concert? No, I was working. It's nearly impossible to succeed in the world and also succeed in the house, which means, at some level, even if you do not realize it, you make a choice. This is a regret. I wish I had been there more, had done better, had given my children as much as my parents gave me. I did not. I was always divided, being pulled away, on the phone, and so forth. But maybe you do best by being true to your nature. Whatever my children have lost to my work habits, they have made back in the privileges afforded them by my success. I could not give them what my parents gave me, so I gave them the world instead.

The Producer

Just what does a movie producer do?

It's a question I hear all the time.

Well, simply put, the producer is a driving force behind the project. It's often the producer who finds the story, the article that reads like a movie, the novel that cries out to be filmed, the event you just know will light up the screen. He tracks down the author or owner or real-life players, secures the rights—at favorable terms—hires a writer to turn the story into a script, which is key. I don't care what kind of cast you have, how beautifully the thing is shot—if you don't have the right script, you're going to fail. But with the right script, you can set yourself up with a studio, get a bucket of cash, hire a great director and actors, scout locations, and so forth. As the project proceeds, your job—one of them, anyway—is to police and guide everything, to be the adult, the voice of authority, the wallet when it's pay time, the hammer when it's hammer time. For this, you take some of the credit when it works, and most of the blame when it fails.

What qualifies a person to be a movie producer?

Another question I'm often asked.

Well, it's mostly a matter of temperament. You have to enjoy being in the world, mixing it up, reveling in hits and misses. A movie set is like Brigadoon, a city that appears on the sands and exists for just a time, with all the rivalries and passions of a metropolis. The producer is mayor of that city, shaking hands and walking streets, calling people to compromise, rise above, and, crucially, to work with people they do not like. You have to praise and you have to scold. It must have been easier in the old days, of course, when the actors were on contract and thus were simply told: Go there, play that. But every player is now a free agent, meaning everyone is a star and expects to get paid like a star, or at least a little bit more than anyone else is getting paid.

This dynamic—everyone measuring himself or herself against everyone else—has just about killed the ensemble picture. *The Wild Bunch, The Dirty Dozen, The Magnificent Seven*— you hardly ever see movies like that anymore. It's become nearly impossible to produce a film with more than three major stars. It's less about money than about politics. People talk on the set, and when they talk, they compare, and when they compare, they bitch. Some demand raises or back-end points, others simply storm off. Which is why I consider the *Ocean's* movies such a triumph. Merely being able to assemble such a cast—Clooney, Pitt, Damon, Gould, Garcia, Cheadle, and so on—and keep it together through three pictures was a feat. My role in this was both as hands-on tactician and as guiding spirit. I was the old man upstairs, saying, "Isn't this fantastic! Can you believe all of the fun we're having?"

But the main job of the producer is this: Solve problems. The list of my movies is, in fact, little more than a list of problems solved. *The pit boss won't let us shoot in the casino? Fine! Build a casino in Burbank.* Each movie tells the story of its producer, where the idea came from, and how the crises were averted.

Take, for example, *Oh, God!,* which I produced after *Nashville.* It was a breakthrough for me. With it, I finally reached the great American middle that Colonel Tom Parker talked about so often. The idea came from David Geffen, who acquired the rights to the novel and wanted to cast John Denver as the lead, a befuddled, latter-day Abraham, who, while managing a supermarket in California, hears the voice of God. It was a perfect part for John and a great way for him to branch out into something new, the average lifespan of a pop star being not much longer than the average career of an NFL running back. Geffen asked me to produce. Larry Gelbart and Carl Reiner were already assigned to write and direct. You could do no better. Gelbart was the author of *A Funny Thing Happened on the Way to the Forum.* Carl Reiner was the creator of *The Dick Van Dyke Show.* The men worked together on Sid Caesar's *Your Show of Shows.* Alan Arkin had been signed to play God, which made sense. Not only is Arkin a great actor, he was friends with Reiner and Gelbart. He was young, though, a little slight for the part of Yahweh. I mean, when you think of God, what do you picture? For me, it's a gray-haired, humorous old Jew, with slumped shoulders and big hands and a cigar in his mouth.

After discussions of a theological nature—*What kind of voice do you think the big guy would have? Do you think the divine would take his own name in vain?*—Reiner and Gelbart and I realized we were all picturing the same face.

All three of us decided the only person for this part was George Burns.

Burns was in his late seventies, a legend with a career that went clear back to the golden age of radio and, before that, to the Yiddish theater. He was a vision of the almighty in modest, human form. He was available, but the situation was tricky. It meant firing Arkin, who was friends with everyone. But when we explained it to him, he understood. The part of God was not one you could use the Method to play—you could not draw on your own experience to get into the mind of the Infinite. You simply had to be an old man who had been around forever, had done everything, had known everyone.

It all came back around years later, when I was casting *Ocean's Eleven*. I signed Arkin to play the part of Saul, who was just the kind of wise, humorous old man Burns would have played a generation before. Two days before shooting, I got a call. Arkin was going in for surgery and would miss the shoot. I was in a panic. I went over to Carl Reiner's house in the middle of the night, banged on the door, handed him the script, and said, "Please, Carl, you have to play the part of Saul in *Ocean's Eleven*."

He said, "Jerry, Jerry, why so late?"

"Well," I told him, "Arkin was supposed to do it, but he's in the hospital."

"Oh, I see," said Carl, "Alan is still not ready to play God."

The table read of *Oh, God!* is still vivid in my mind. This is the first real rehearsal: The producer and director and writer sit around as the actors go through the entire script, playing their parts for the first time. It's early in the process, but usually, from how the actors work together and react, you can get a sense of how the movie will play. George Burns entered in that slow, shuffling way of his—every step made me laugh. He was seventy-nine, impossibly old. Who knew he would live another twenty years? His face was like parchment. His eyes were warm and dark. He wore an obvious toupee—it was the one off note. He was a great performer. Everyone stood when he came in. For the actors, reading with him was like taking batting practice with Babe Ruth. But he was an old man, so you could not help but wonder how he would handle his lines. When we started reading, though, it was obvious he knew not only his part, but every part in the script. If John Denver fumbled, George Burns would correct him. He was incredible. Before the read, he talked with Gelbart and Reiner and Avery Corman, who wrote the novel. He went through the script with a pen, explaining which lines would hit and which would bomb, which would get big laughs and which would get embarrassed snickers. "You will kill with this one," he said, "but with this one, you'll wonder if you picked the wrong profession."

Making the movie was a dream. The only issue, really, was George's hair, or, to be specific, fake hair. Simply put, he would not take off his toupee. We begged, *please, for this role, ditch it.* He refused. It was a question for priests and rabbis. Would the Lord of Hosts wear a piece? To me, the answer was obvious. Even if God is bald, or has a bald spot, and even if this makes him self-conscious when he walks upon the earth, don't you think that, rather than getting a rug, he would just make new hair? I mean, if he could part the waters...? But Burns refused, which meant a movie in which God would wear a rug. No good. As I said, the job of the producer is to solve problems. I therefore decreed: *The Lord will wear a hat!* If you watch the movie, you will see that God is pictured, variously, in a baseball hat, a cowboy hat, a captain's hat. He is a man of many moods and many seasons.

The movie was finished. I was convinced we had a smash. But when I showed it to the business people at Warner Bros., they sat through it politely, without comment.

Well, yes, they said when it was done, *it's a nice little picture.*

Nice little picture? *No, I said, it's a great film. But it will be huge only if we treat it like it's huge.* I said I wanted five million dollars to market it on television. They told me I was insane. Back then, no one advertised movies on TV. "Look, TV is where John Denver is a star," I told them. "It's where his fans are. You show them the movie, and let them know about it, you will have a monster hit on your hands." They told me to go away. The movie had cost less than two million dollars to make. There was no way they were going to chase that two million with five million for commercials.

I spoke to Terry Semel, who was the head of distribution at Warners—he wound up running the company—and Andy Fogelson, who was the head of marketing. I made them watch the movie again, then argued my case. They fell in love with it. They went in to their bosses and said, "Give Jerry the money." They put their jobs on the line. Terry said, "If this fails, I'll quit the company." It was a huge moment for me and Terry—we've been friends ever since. We went on television with the biggest ad campaign Hollywood had ever seen, found John's fans, and hit them squarely, the result being a summer of packed theaters. We made history.

While making the movie, I became friendly with George Burns. Jane and I decided to throw a party for his eightieth birthday at our house in Beverly Hills. For that one night, the world was as I had always imagined it. Invitations went out by hand: black-and-white cards with a red rose. The party was catered by Chasen's. Dinner on the tennis court, dozens of tables under white cloths, torches and tiki lamps, a jazz band. Frank Sinatra, Kirk Douglas, Cary Grant, Gene Kelly, Johnny Carson, everyone was there. As Louis B. Mayer used to say, "More stars than in the heavens." At one point, Groucho Marx got up for an impromptu roast of George Burns. Groucho was old and failing, but he was brilliant. Goddamn, he was funny. It was Groucho's last public performance. The party went all night. When I came downstairs in the morning, I found the young stars of Hollywood passed out on the floor, some of whom had won Grammies or Golden Globes the night before. They were in their suits, hugging their statues, snoring away.

Or take, for example, *Cruising*—another set of problems solved—which I made after *Oh, God!*. It's the story of a New York cop who goes undercover in the gay leather bars of New York to solve a series of murders. It was based on a true story, having first been reported in a series of articles in the *New York Times*. I bought the rights to the book that came out of the articles, put the screenplay in a drawer, and waited for the right moment.

Meanwhile, I hooked up with director Billy Friedkin, who had just come off the career-making success of *The Exorcist*. We became friends, decided to make a movie together. Then, one night, as we were talking, I remembered *Cruising*. I got the book out of my drawer, handed it to Billy. "Look at this," I said. "It might be for you." He knew the story, having followed it in the paper.

"I love this," he said. "We're making this movie."

We met with Frank Wells, who was then vice chairman of Warners. We pitched the movie. He signed off on it without understanding what he was signing off on. He probably thought it was about cars. Billy and I were so hot at that moment—*Oh, God!, The Exorcist*—that he just said "Yeah, yeah, do it." Then, just before we were to begin shooting, Wells suddenly figured out the movie was not about cars. There would be controversy, noise. He told us Warners could not make the movie. I was in a fury. We had already begun to rehearse, but Wells did not care. It was a bad moment, but in the end we managed to set up the movie at Lorimar Pictures.

A few years had passed since the book was published, and in those few years, the world had changed. The gay community had begun its liberation. People were coming out of the closet. In hopes of getting it right, Billy and I hit all the leather bars of the West Village, then shot the movie in these locations. A reporter from the *Village Voice* got the script early, then infiltrated the set, where he heard wild rumors, the result being a hysterical article that denounced the film, denounced Billy, and denounced me. It said we were exploiting the gay community, that lives would be put in danger. That it was all bullshit was beside the point. Being in the newspaper made it true. As I said, the job of the producer is solving problems, and this was a big one: Just like that, our sleepy set had turned into a riot scene. Thousands of people came out to protest. They stomped their feet, flashed lights, and blew whistles when we were trying to shoot. We burned up thousands of dollars in film. Then the letters came: *You're dead. We're going to kill you, Weintraub.* Garbage like that. I did not mind the threats. In this case, my job was to be the loudmouth, the target, take the hit and let the fury of the mob break over my head, giving the actors room to perform. I mean, we had Al Pacino, and it's hard to do the Method while you're being filmed for the five-o'clock news.

In the end, the press was good for the movie. The articles sold the product. One day, Steve Ross, who was the CEO of Warner Bros.' parent company, Warner Communications, and also a friend, said to me, "Wow, Jerry, you are getting so much attention with the picture. Why aren't *we* doing it?"

I told him the whole story.

He said something like, *Well, whatever you want to make next, we want to be involved.*

Cruising came out in 1980. It did well at the box office, pushed along by all that coverage. Of course, the movie, in many ways, came too early. If it was released today, when people have opened their minds to lifestyles that differ from their own, it would do gangbusters. As I always say, "Better too late than too early." Too late means you look slow but still make a bundle. Too early means you look like you've lost your mind, and you get people shouting, "Kill that idiot." But it also means there is a chance for rediscovery. In the end, that strange little picture we made in the seventies became a cult classic.

Soon after that, Friedkin said, "That was so much fun, let's do it again."

"Do what again?" I asked.

"Make another picture."

"Do you have anything in mind?"

"Yeah," he said. "Let's make a sequel to *The Exorcist.*"

As an idea, this was automatic. He could have made it with any producer, but if you need a person to deal with studio executives and budgets and marketers and minutiae, well, I'm not a bad choice. Directors know I'm on their side of the table. I will fight for them, make their case, protect them. William Peter Blatty was a partner, as he owned the rights. And he would, of course, write the sequel. He had done such a brilliant job with the original as well as the novel it was based on.

Frank Wells got word of the project. He called and said, "Look, Jerry, I want it."

"After what you did to me on *Cruising*?" I said. "No way."

"You've got to let me have it," he said. "If we don't get it, it will kill my career with Steve Ross."

Frank Wells and I were actually friends—I did not want to hurt the guy.

He said, "Go to your office in the morning. There will be an envelope waiting. Look inside, then call me."

"What is it?"

"Just get the envelope, then call me."

I went in and there was the envelope. Inside was a check for five hundred thousand dollars.

I called Wells.

"What's it for?" I asked.

"Just to be the first to hear the pitch," he said.

"And what happens if you hate the pitch?" I asked.

"Tell me the budget," he said.

"Fifteen million," I said, pulling the number out of thin air.

"Good," he said. "Come in and tell us the story. If we approve, the five hundred thousand is against the budget. If we don't approve, you keep the money."

How can you beat that?

I scheduled a meeting for New York three weeks hence, where we would sit with the heads of Warner Bros. and pitch. I call it the five-hundred-thousand-dollar lunch, because that's all they got for their money—lunch with me and Billy and Blatty.

It's interesting that no one questioned my decision to have that lunch in New York. We all lived in LA—writer, director, producer, all the executives—so why were we flying across the country for a meeting? Well, the fact is, I could not get these guys to agree on a scenario for the movie, so I figured, okay, we'll be stuck together for five hours on the plane. That is when Friedkin and Blatty will work it out. In fact, they did not work it out, and could never agree. By the time we landed, I knew we were in serious trouble.

When we got to Warner Bros., the receptionist told me that Mr. Ross wanted to see me right away. I went in, we spoke. He said, "Jerry, we're buying this movie."

I said, "Buying what? There's no story."

He said, "Well, go and make one up. We're doing this movie."

We went into the meeting, sat at the big table with the food piled in front of us. Ted Ashley and Frank Wells, the chairman and vice chairman of the company, were both in the room. For the first thirty minutes, it was just me, telling Sinatra stories, telling Elvis stories, telling Dean Martin stories, the whole routine.

Frank Wells finally turned to Billy and said, "Okay, Billy, why don't you tell us about your movie?"

Billy bumbled around a bit, then said, "We open in the hills of West Virginia, and the camera comes over the hills and we see a field of dead cows. The camera continues over a hill, and we see Washington, D.C., Georgetown, go up the steps and into a church, then we see a head, severed and bloody, roll out of the confessional."

He turned to Blatty, then said, "Take it, Bill."

"Well, yes," said Blatty, "but I am not sure about the cows."

Then it was over. As we were getting ready to leave, Frank Wells helped me on with my coat. "We're excited," he told me. "We can't wait to make this movie."

"What movie?" I asked him. "There is no movie. That was bullshit."

"No, no, we love it," he said. "We want to do it."

"There is nothing to do," I said. "I'm going to give back your money."

"No, hang on to it," he said. "Think about it."

Well, I did think about it, and the more I thought about it, the more I knew there was no movie. I sent back the money with a note: "Next time." Taking money for a movie you know you will never make is a bad habit. It's cocaine, it revs you up, and you have some fun, but in the end, you're in a worse place than you were when you started.

Around this time, my parents visited Beverly Hills. This was rare, as my mother did not like to fly. Usually I visited them in New York. The trip was therefore a big deal, a chance to show off what I had accomplished. I picked them up at LAX in my chauffer-driven Rolls-Royce. My mother slid in slowly, beaming, but my father looked skeptical. He stared out the window as we drove, now and then asking things like, "How long have you had this car, Jerry?" "What's the miles per gallon?" We finally reached the house, the mansion in Beverly Hills, with the swimming pool and tennis court and gardens and flowers. We sat in the living room. Out came the champagne. Out came the caviar. My mother was enjoying every minute. My father was reserved, pensive. He was a warm and beautiful man. I handed him a Cuban cigar, a Cohiba, his favorite. He puffed at it, looking at the smoke.

"Go get ready," I said. "I have a dinner planned. I am taking you to the best place in town, where the stars hang out."

This went on for a few days—me giving my parents the business, ushering them to the front of lines, through crowds, to the best tables and shows, and so on—until my father finally said, "Okay, listen, Jerry, I want to talk to you. Let's go outside."

Before we got halfway down the front steps, he tapped my chest with his finger and said, "I want to ask you a question, and I want you to tell me the truth, no bullshit from you. Are you in the Mafia? How did you get all this? You were never that smart.'"

I stammered. "Uh, no, Dad, I'm creative. I did it."

"Well, where's your inventory?" he asked. "How can you have this much money and not have an inventory? It doesn't make sense to me."

I laughed and pointed at my head. "It's up here," I said. "All the inventory is right up here."

Then he laughed, too, saying, "Well, I guess there was always a lot of space for it, anyway."

That trip was mostly about impressing my mother, showing her a good time, thanking her. It was my mother who instilled the confidence and belief that made my success possible. My mother had two great passions in her life (other than her family, I mean): Cary Grant and horse races. So one afternoon, a week into the trip, I tell her to get ready, we're going somewhere—I won't say where. Thirty minutes later, the Rolls drops us off at the Hollywood Park Race Track. As we're getting out, who does she spot but Cary Grant, elegant as always, standing in front of the ticket window. "Oh, my," says my mother, grabbing my sleeve. "Look who it is." Before she can get his name out, Cary hurries over and slips his hand through my mother's arm and says, "Hello, Rose, will you be my date this afternoon?"

By then, Cary and I had become friends. I must have told my parents this on the phone, but they probably did not believe me. My mother was walking on air. They sat together in the clubhouse, reading through the racing form. Cary made her bets. They watched the ponies through binoculars.

I threw a dinner party that night at the house. I was sitting at the bar, having a drink with my mother, when Sinatra came in. There was always a stir, a happy little party, whenever Frank entered a room. He threw off his coat and came up, smiling, with his arms outstretched. "Hi ya, Rose," he said, "I heard you had a great date for lunch today."

"Yes, I did," she told him—and this part chokes me up, because my parents, well, that was a real love affair, "but I like my Sammy better."

My mother, as I said, was one of those ladies you would see weeping in a dark theater on the Grand Concourse. She loved the movies. In 1986, I actually had a chance to take her out of the seats and put her up on screen. My parents had come to visit me in Florida, where I was making a movie called *Happy New Year* with Peter Falk, Tom Courtenay, and Charles Durning.

After the director, John Avildsen, met my mother, he said, "Hey, Jerry, why don't you put her in the movie?"

The picture was about a jewelry store robbery, and I built the store on set. Avildsen thought I should have her in the scene in which Falk cases the joint. She would be a customer, walking by with Courtenay, the store manager.

"Not a good idea," I told Avildsen.

"Why?"

"It's my mother," I said. "Believe me. It's not a good idea."

"Come on, Jerry, she'll enjoy herself."

Falk and Avildsen kidded me into it.

So I went over and said, "Mom, do you want to be in the scene, you could be an extra."

"No," she said. "I'm no actress."

"Okay," I said, "understood." And I walked away.

A minute later, she called me back.

"What is it, Ma?

"Jerry," she said, "if you need me, I'll do it."

(She was a real Jewish mother.)

I said, "No, no, it's okay."

She said, "Just look at you. I can tell you need me. Fine. I'll do it. But I don't have a dress, look at what I'm wearing. And my hair…"

I said, "Ma, I got a wardrobe truck, I got hairdressers, I got makeup people. You'll be fine."

"Oh, you're going to do all that?"

Yes.

She said, "All right, I'll do it for you."

So she goes in, is treated like a queen, like she's Julia Roberts or Marilyn Monroe. The hairdresser, the makeup people, they're all working on her. Now comes time for her scene. She comes out in the background and is supposed to walk out the door. So Avildsen says to me, "Why don't you direct it? It's your mother."

I said, "No, don't be crazy."

He said, "What do you have to do? Say 'action'? Say 'cut'? Everything is set up, don't worry. It'll be fun for her."

I said, "Okay, okay."

Then: "Action!"

My mother and Tom Courtenay start walking. She's supposed to go from here to there. But as she passes, she turns to Courtenay and says, "I don't like that piece of jewelry."

I yelled, "Cut! Cut! Cut!"

I said, "Ma, what are you doing? There's no lines. You just walk."

"Well that's stupid," she said. "If your father was showing some jewelry to somebody and she didn't like it, she'd tell him."

"Well, in this case, you don't tell him anything," I said. "You just walk."

"It's stupid," she told me. "I wouldn't do it that way."

"But it's not about you, Ma. It's about Peter Falk."

Meanwhile, Peter Falk and John Avildsen, and all the Teamsters, are standing around, watching me, laughing their asses off.

So I went back, and said, "Okay, let's do it again. Action."

She started walking, then, just as she passed the camera, she turned, looked right into the lens, and smiled like a bandit.

"Cut! Cut! Cut!"

"What's the matter now?" she asked.

I said, "Ma, you're embarrassing me."

I'm talking quietly because I don't want everybody to hear. They are all looking, and they know I'm screwed. No way I'm getting out of this without pain.

I said, "Ma, listen to me, please. I feel like I'm back in sixth grade. You're killing me. I'm supposed to be in charge and you're making me a child. My mother, standing on the set, telling me I'm stupid, telling me what to do. You can't do that."

She said, "Well, it doesn't make sense."

I said, "Ma, do me a favor, please? Just walk from there to there. Don't look at the camera, don't say anything, just walk."

"Fine," she said, "I was doing this for you but it's not right."

We finally finished. I was exhausted. It took all day. We got back to the hotel. Jane said, "You know, you should invite your mom to the dailies."

"No, not a good idea."

"Oh, come on," said Jane. "Let her see herself. It will be a thrill."

So I called. "Ma, do you want to watch the dailies in the morning?"

"What's dailies?"

"It's everything we shot today," I told her. "We take a look at it. Your film will be on the screen. You want to see it?"

"You want me to come to dailies?" she said. "No. I don't want to see myself, I don't care about that, it's silly."

I said, "Okay, good night."

Hung up.

A minute later, the phone rang. "All right, if you need me to come, I'll come," she said. "And I can see that you need me."

She brought my father. Peter Falk found out and he came, too. Same with John Avildsen, Tom Courtenay, and Charlie Durning—they were all there. My mother was sitting next to me. When she came on screen, she yelled out, "I look great!"

In the end, she loved it, mostly because she got residual checks from the film—$3, $27, $41—for years and years.

Leaving on a Jet Plane

By 1977, John Denver was the biggest star in the world. This was no accident. It was, in fact, the result of a carefully orchestrated campaign to package and sell him, as I had packaged and sold weekend getaways in the window of the Sachs Men's Shop in Fairbanks. I tried everything with John, sold him in every way I knew how. One year, for example, he was late with an album, had missed a deadline for Christmas, which infuriated the executives at RCA. They wanted their record or their money. It was John's ass. "Jerry," he said, "what can we do?"

"Don't worry," I told him. "We'll fix it."

I designed an album cover, pasted it on envelopes, and sent it to record stores. You bought the envelope, which could be traded for the album, making you an inside player, an investor in Denver's career. It was a gimmick that worked. The envelopes sold like mad—a perfect gift for the John Denver fan in your life. The record went gold before it even existed. I went to RCA and said, "Look, you've had your Christmas, now where's our money?"

And yet, for various reasons, John began to lose his bearings. It's a danger of success: You're a kid, and want only to be heard; then you are heard, by everybody, all the time, but your thought is, either, "Well, yeah, great, but now what?" or "Yes, they hear me, but it's not the real me, not the voice I have in my head, or the person I want to be."

There were portents and signs. John started talking about ditching his glasses, his earnest and trustworthy glasses. He wanted to change his hair, too, which would be like Nike ditching its swoop. His hair and his glasses were known and loved everywhere on earth. Probably even the Bushmen of Africa could hum a few bars of "Rocky Mountain High." Then, coming off the huge success of *Oh, God!*, which set him up for a major career in film, I developed a follow-up, *An Officer and a Gentleman*, which John turned down. He said it was a B movie, and not good enough for him with its seedy backdrop of desolate airstrips and Panhandle bars. Of course, *An Officer and a Gentleman* was not only a great film, but also the movie that really launched the career of Richard Gere.

Much of this confusion had to do with problems in his own life, ways in which, so it seemed to him, everything was coming apart. First of all, his marriage had ended. He had split with Annie, who wasn't just his childhood sweetheart, but his muse. Much of his desire for her, the chase and courtship, could be heard, sublimated, in his best songs. The end of the marriage was the end of his life, the first life he lived from the time he left home. Then his father died. He had trouble with his father, but they had been close at the end. These losses hit him hard. In fact, the only person left from his old life was me. Which explains a lot. The man was trying to reinvent himself, start again by forgetting. This is when I began to hear rumors: John is upset. John is unhappy. John wants to leave you.

I discounted these, because, I mean, look what we had

done together: in the ten years since I found him, this obscure, underpaid nightclub singer had become one of the biggest stars in the world, with hit records and shows and a big movie career before him, and money pouring in. But I did not realize how troubled he was, how insecure, and how badly he ached to be free. This was my friend, the executor of my will, the caretaker of my (God forbid) orphaned children, yet I knew nothing about him. That you know a person, does not mean you know a person.

So one morning, I was sitting in my office on Wilshire Boulevard—I had a huge office, with a million-dollar view of the hills—when John came storming in, unannounced and unplanned, a freight train with a head of steam.

"We have to talk, Jerry."

"Hey, John," I said, "great to see you. How're you doing?"

"Fine, fine," he said. "I've got something to tell you."

"Okay, good, tell me."

"I'm firing you."

I sat back and looked at him. I was infuriated, enraged. Look at this guy. Look where he was and look where he is. And now he comes here like this, not even sitting, not even talking and explaining, to tell me it's over and we are done. At such moments, I don't know why, my gut instinct is, *Hey, fuck you!*

"What did you say?" I asked.

"I'm firing you."

"Can you repeat that?"

"I'm firing you, Jerry."

I came out from behind the desk, came at him like you would come at someone on a basketball court. I was really hot. "Say it again," I told him. "I want to hear you say it again."

"I'm firing you."

"I don't ever want to see your face again," I told him. "Get out of my office. Who the fuck do you think you are?"

"Don't you want to know why I'm firing you?" he asked.

"I don't care why, what, where, or how," I said. "Don't ever say my name again in your lifetime; get out of here."

I threw him out. I went over to the window and stared at the hills without seeing, the blood pulsing in my face.

Later that afternoon, John's business manager called to tell me that all the things I owned with John—we were partners on every show and record—no longer belonged to me, as I had been booking his shows while also working as a producer, which was not permitted, or some such mumbo jumbo. I could hardly follow him, and I did not care. I was angry, heartbroken as well. "What's the point of this conversation?" I asked. "Just tell me what you're trying to tell me."

He said, "You don't own anything with John anymore."

I said, "I don't want to own anything with John. You can keep it all." And I hung the phone up.

I was depressed for weeks. Not about losing a client but about losing a friend, somebody to whom I had given so much of myself.

Things did not go well for John after that. RCA dropped him, his talent agency dropped him, most of the other people he worked with dropped him. I knew all of them and they understood how the operation functioned. What we created with John, the persona, the mood, simply was not real; we invented it. We were so interwoven, there was simply no way you could have Denver without Weintraub—not as John Denver had been in the seventies. It was his talent, but it was also my maneuvering. I was really his partner in everything. I did all the marketing and press. I packaged and sold him and turned him into a star. I put in a lot of my own money and all of my effort and ingenuity, because he was so talented and because I loved him. I still do. I miss him even now. When John died—in 1997, he crashed an experimental aircraft off the California coast—there was still so much left to do, to forgive and to be forgiven for, but who knows. As the poets say, death is not a period, it's an ellipsis.

John and I did not talk for years. He was just another star dimming in the glassy firmament, another face on TV. I wanted to forget him. Because he had been such a good friend, because the end had been so traumatic, because he had hurt me. I buried it and moved on. I did not see him again until 1984, in a restaurant at the Olympics in Sarajevo, Yugoslavia. We exchanged polite hellos. Cordial, but cold.

"Hey, Jerry," he asked, "now do you want to hear why I fired you?"

"No, John," I told him, "I honestly don't give a fuck."

Then, finally, about ten years after that, we ran into each other again and this time, probably because so many years had gone by, we could finally talk calmly.

"Now do you want to hear why I fired you?" he asked.

"No, not really," I said, "because I don't think there can be a good reason, but if you have something you need to say, then just say it."

"Then I will tell you why I fired you," he said. "Because finally, after the death of my father and the end of my marriage, I wanted to take charge of my own life. I knew I could never do that while you were running my affairs. More than a manager and a friend, you were a father. And I had to see if I could live a life without fathers. I mean, Jerry, you ran my whole life!"

I clapped him on the shoulder and I said, "Yeah, but did I really do such a bad job of it? Was it really so terrible?"

Knowing Which Calls to Return

O ne morning, at the end of the 1970s, I got into the office early. I like being up when New York is just waking, the old metabolism still governing in the Pacific Time Zone. I like knowing I have done an entire day of work before the clock strikes nine. When my secretary came in, she handed me the call list.

Now, let me explain my call list of those years: Simply put, it was the names and numbers of all the people who had called and whom I was obligated to call back, three or four pages typed up and handed to me each morning. These names, taken together, told the story of my day: managers looking to cut deals, studio executives looking to pitch scenarios, actors looking for representation, arena owners wanting to renegotiate a split, politicians looking for a handout, rock stars angered by a missing amenity or anemic sound system, local promoters apoplectic over a perceived infringement, reporters looking for a quotation, bankers looking to sell bonds, realtors looking to sell or buy land, clients panicked between projects, friends looking for tickets or a room in a sold-out hotel in Vegas—hotels are never really sold out.

So my secretary gave me the list—all these calls were in

regard to Concerts West, my music business—and, as I was paging through the names, I suddenly realized that I did not want to call back any of these people. I sat there for a moment, thinking about what this meant, what my gut was telling me. It was not making the calls that bothered me. It was *having* to make the calls. In a flash I thought, I will quit this business instead of making these calls. I don't feel that way about my call list now—being successful means filling your life with calls you want to return. But in that moment, I knew that period of my life had ended. I was done with being a manager, because when you are a manager, you're not working for yourself. You're working for the people on the list. I'm not knocking it. But I just didn't want to work for anyone else. I called my clients over the next few days. I told them, one by one, "I love ya, find someone else, I'm done."

All these years later, people still ask me how I was able to walk away from the concert business.

"Don't you regret it? There was so much money to be made."

"Not for a minute," I tell them. "Not for a second."

You have to be willing to walk away from the most comfortable perch, precisely because it is the most comfortable.

The next morning was the greatest morning of my life. I went to the office at the usual hour, had my coffee, read my paper, and did my work as usual, only this time, when my secretary came in with the call list, I crossed out the names of all the people I did not want to call back. I was free! There was nobody I had to talk to. It was so liberating. I had become my own person.

Do you understand what I'm saying?

Irving Azoff is one of the most successful men I know. He

is a dear friend. He is as big and rich and brilliant as they come. But Irving Azoff has clients. One of his clients calls, he has to call back. Me? I call back who I want, when I want. That's freedom.

In this way, I became a full-time movie producer. It was all I did, all I wanted to do. I was a free agent in search of ideas, combing the ether for projects, looking to put scenarios together with writers, to put writers together with directors, directors together with actors, all the time trying to match the feats of my heroes Mike Todd and Billy Wilder and Louis B. Mayer. In my memory, those years play as a succession of movies, each dating my life the way a layer of sediment dates an era of civilization. One of my favorites was *Diner*, which I made in 1982. It's about a group of friends passing the last days of their youth in the parking lots and row houses of Baltimore. It was written by Barry Levinson, who, at that point, was known only as a writer, having worked on several movies with Mel Brooks.

I got the screenplay on a Friday at 8:00 A.M. By 9:30, I had fallen in love. Every kid I grew up with—the sports nut, the married-too-early, the deviant maniac—was in that script. You couldn't be from the East Coast and literate and not understand those guys. They came off the pages.

I called Levinson.

I said, "I have to make this movie."

"Great," he said, "but you do know that every studio in town has already turned it down?"

"I don't care what they did," I told him. "I love this movie and I'm going to make it."

"Great," he said, "and I'm going to direct it."

"Whoa! Wait a second. I did not know that was part of the deal."

"Yeah," he said, "it is."

Levinson had never directed before, and the script, as he said, had already been turned down. But if you think about it, and I did think about it, this really was his story, his life, and his world: Who could possibly tell it better than him?

"Okay," I said, "as long as I have the right to fire you, I don't care if you direct."

Barry, who had great faith in himself, agreed.

I went all over town with the script, pitched like mad, but no one was interested. It's nearly impossible to sell a story that has no grand concept, reads intimate and small, and is moody in the way a song can be moody—you get it or don't. It was like trying to sell jazz to a person who's never heard Coltrane. Finally, when I was about to give up, David Chasman, an executive at MGM who could really read a script, called.

"How much is this going to cost?"

"Five and a half million dollars."

"We're on."

The key to *Diner* was casting. For this, credit goes to Ellen Chenoweth, who is one of the greatest casting directors of all time. She understood the script and was able to find real-life equivalents of the characters, clearly based on real guys, among the hungry young actors of LA. My job was to see what Levinson saw, then sell the executives at MGM on a cast of unknowns.

It's no accident that, in the course of my life, I've launched dozens of careers. Like my father, I can look at a sea of sapphires and pick out the Star of Ardaban: the young kid who will blossom on stage, glow on screen, separate from the journeymen to become a star. *Diner* launched, among others, Ellen Barkin, Mickey Rourke, Kevin Bacon, Daniel Stern, and Steve Guttenberg.

Another favorite of those years was *September 30, 1955*, about the day James Dean died. It, too, was brilliantly cast, marking the debut of Tom Hulce and Dennis Quaid. That it did not find an audience is a perplexing mystery. Wise men say you learn more from failure than from success, and, though that's often true, in this case failure left me nothing but confused. So many variables determine the fate of a film, some having to do with script and casting and marketing; but others are so mysterious and zeitgeist-related and beyond human control that the best posture is humility. There are three key words in business: *I don't know.*

Ideas come from many places. Sometimes they arrive in the mail as a script. Sometimes they develop like stalagmites, growing from a slow drip of thoughts. Sometimes they appear on TV, as a story in the news. Take, for example, *The Karate Kid.* I was at home watching the five-o'clock news. All the stations were broadcasting the same story. It was about a kid in the Valley who had been getting beat up every day on his way home from school. He took it and took it, until, tired of taking it, he found a teacher and learned karate. The next time the bullies came, it was lights out for the bad guys. I loved the story. It reminded me of the ninety-pound weakling ads they used to have for Charles Atlas.

I found the kid. Billy Sassner. I had a car pick up him and his parents and bring them to my office. His dad was heavy-set, a postman. His mom was heavy, too. (We made her a character in the first movie, but wrote her out of the sequels; the actress wanted too much money. I told the writer, "Deal with it in the script." It was going to be a funeral or a phone call—the phone call was cheaper.) I told Billy's parents just what I wanted to do, then made a deal for the rights to their story. I hired a screenwriter named Robert Kamen, who, in addition to being really good, knew all about karate, which was, of course, a huge advantage in writing the fight scenes.

The plot was classic—the picked-on kid takes his revenge and the bully gets his comeuppance—but I wanted the movie to be more. Kamen and I knew it was not about karate, not really. It was about fathers and sons. Since the kid has no father in the film, this wise old teacher, this Japanese man named Miyagi, becomes his father. We worked hard to get that right. A lot of Miyagi is, in fact, my father, everybody's father, if not the father you had, then the father you wish you had.

I hired John Avildsen to direct. He had won the Academy Award for *Rocky*, and *The Karate Kid* was really just *Rocky* in another way—it was an underdog story, a Cinderella story and a fantasy, the world as you wish it would be. We signed Ralph Macchio to play the kid, then found the girl. How does the girl fit into the picture? Haven't you ever been to the movies? There's always a girl in the picture! I found her in a Burger King commercial. She jumped off the screen. This was Elisabeth Shue, who later became a star in her own right.

We soon had every major part cast with the exception of Miyagi, the most important part in the movie—the father, the teacher, the moral center, heart, and soul. I went to Hong Kong. I went to Kabuki theaters in Kyoto. I traveled the world looking for this guy. It was a manhunt. I flew the great Japanese actor Toshiro Mifune to LA. He showed up at my office with twenty-five or thirty people. He looked great, but something did not seem right. Whenever I asked him a question, a member of his entourage answered.

"How do you like the script?"

"Mr. Mifune likes the script very much."

"How do you like your green tea?"

"Mr. Mifune likes his green tea very much."

I threw everyone out but Mifune.

I said, "I want to talk to Toshiro myself."

They went out reluctantly, looking back, but they went.

I closed the door and said, "No bullshit now. Do you speak English?"

"No," he said, "not really."

"Then how can I do this picture with you?"

He said he could sound out the lines phonetically—it would sound all right, even if he did not know the meaning of the words.

"No, no," I said, "we can't do that."

Mifune went to Western Costume after the meeting and had pictures of himself taken dressed as Miyagi. I still have them. He looked fantastic. He was a strong man. I was tempted, but how can you play father-and-son scenes phonetically? I called the director John Frankenheimer, who worked with Mifune in *Grand Prix*.

"How did you do it?"

He told me they shot him in Japanese, went back, and dubbed all his lines into English. I did not have the budget for that. Mifune was out.

I believe in not getting hung up or paralyzed in a quest for perfection, but by the same token, you have to identify what is truly important and hold out until you can get those things right: Miyagi was important. And I could not find him. I was about to put the picture on hold. We would just have to wait until fate brought us Miyagi-san.

Then, one morning, John Avildsen burst into my office, grinning as if he had just made the mother of all breakthroughs, as if he had just found the cure for old age.

"I know who should play Miyagi," he said.

"Who?"

"Pat Morita."

"Pat Morita?"

"Yeah, Pat Morita."

I knew Pat Morita. I knew him when I was busing tables up in the Catskills. He was a hundred-dollar-a-night comic at the resorts. He played a character called "The Hip Nip." He came onstage in horn-rimmed glasses and fake buck teeth and, in a bad Japanese accent, from an old World War II movie, said, "Don't forget Pearl Harbor."

I told John Avildsen, "No. This is a major motion picture. I'm not casting Hip Nip."

"He's great," said Avildsen. "Let him audition at least."

"No fucking way," I said. "Get out of my office."

A few days later I was at my desk, eating a pastrami sandwich and drinking a Dr. Brown's cream soda, when Avildsen barged in, shut the door, and locked it behind him.

"What's this?" I asked.

He put a videotape in the machine and said, "Just watch."

"Why?"

"It's only three minutes. Just watch!"

On came Pat Morita in costume as Miyagi, doing a monologue from the script. "Not bad," I said. "Really, not bad at all."

"Well?" asked Avildsen.

"All right," I said. "Call him up. We'll do a screen test."

We staged a test with Morita and Macchio, a scene in which the kid, who has been hurt, is in bed and Miyagi is nursing him. We shot it. And while we were shooting, I started to cry. I mean, real goddamn tears. The next day, as we were looking at the footage, I said to Avildsen, "You were right, so very right."

Morita was nominated for an Academy Award for his performance in the movie.

No matter how hard you work on a movie, no matter how good you think it is, you never know how it's going to play. You have to wait for the first real audiences, an often endless purgatory of hoping and fearing. With *The Karate Kid*, the waiting ended in a moment of sheer joy. This was at a screening in LA a few weeks before the release. We hung around the lobby talking when the picture was over, then went to the parking lot. Most of the people had gone, but there were forty or fifty kids out there, with their arms outstretched and legs up, imitating the crane kick that comes at the climax of the movie. I knew right then that the picture was going to be a smash.

Arm and Hammer

Armand Hammer had one of the most colorful biographies of the last century. His father, Julius, a Russian immigrant, headed the Communist Party in New York, which was unusual in that the family was quite prosperous. They owned a pharmaceutical company in the Bronx, but there was a scandal. I'm not sure of the details, but it had something to do with an illegal abortion and the death of a young woman. The family was horrified. Julius was sent to Sing Sing. If you're the son of a convict, the middle of three boys, it can have an effect.

Hammer graduated from Columbia medical school, but he never practiced. Still, he loved it when people called him "Dr. Hammer."

When he got out of school, the Russian revolution was in full bloom. There was a lot of suffering. Armand, who knew many of the Soviet leaders through his father—they visited the house on trips to America—decided something had to be done. He got hold of an old ship and filled it with medical supplies, which he took to the Soviets. I don't believe this was done as altruistically as Hammer claimed. I think he was actually unloading stuff his father could not sell. Nevertheless, Lenin heard about the shipments, this great act of charity, and asked to meet with "Dr. Hammer."

This was in the early 1920s, the Lenin of the black-and-white photos, peasant cap worn low, riding the crest of a terrifying wave. And here was Hammer, the son of the disgraced capitalist, shaking hands with Rasputin. Hammer used to say he was the only person who had been friends with both Lenin and Reagan; that was the scope of his life. Lenin thanked Hammer for all he had done, then asked if he wanted to help some more.

"Sure," said Hammer. "What do you need?"

"We have to do business in America," said Lenin. "We need to make deals with all your great men, Henry Ford, the bankers, the financiers. Why don't you represent us, take care of us?"

"Sure," said Hammer.

"And we want to pay you for the medical supplies," said Lenin. "But not in money."

He told Hammer to go to the Hermitage Museum and take whatever he wanted. Hammer went through the halls with a pointer, looking at masterpieces—he knew nothing about art—saying, "Give me two of those, and I'll take one of those, and that one of the monk in the red velvet robe, and that one of the dog." Rembrandts, Pissarros, Cézannes, Fabergé eggs—he got them all. You can see his collection today at the Hammer Museum in LA. There is a curator and there are catalogues and shows and students writing dissertations, but this is how it started, with Hammer, trailed by a minder from the special police, going through the Hermitage, saying, "Give me one of that, give me two of that, give me three of that."

Armand Hammer made a fortune with the Soviets. For several years, he was the only conduit to the West, and thus had a piece of every industry.

The men around Lenin complained. *Who is this American? It doesn't look right! He's getting too much.* Lenin brought Hammer back to Moscow. He said, "Look, Armand, you can't have everything. Pick one business, one industry, and it will be yours."

"One industry?"

"Yes, one industry."

"Okay," said Hammer, "let me think about it."

And he went away, thought about it, and when he came back, he said, "Pencils."

"Pencils?" asked Lenin.

"Yes," said Hammer, "pencils. You've got millions and millions of people in this country, millions of them in school, and every one of them is going to need a pencil."

That was Hammer—head in the clouds, feet on the ground. He thought of basics, of important, everyday things.

Pencils? I mean, we're into big history here, Vladimir Ilyich Lenin, the man who overthrew the czars who defeated Napoleon who succeeded the Sun King and the rest, and what is Hammer thinking about? Pencils!

Hammer went to Germany, where he met with the executives of the Eberhard-Faber Company. He took a group of them back to Russia, where they set up a pencil factory. Hammer made every pencil in the Soviet Union.

By the time I met Hammer, which was decades later, he was on a first-name basis with the most powerful men in the world. He believed that personality could overcome anything, that a great man, by force of will, could straddle every divide—that's why he loved Lenin as much as he loved Reagan. Hammer was the CEO of Occidental Petroleum. This was typical of his luck and his life: The company was not meant to make money at all. He founded it as a tax shelter in the 1960s. Then, a foreman sank a tax shelter drill into an actual oil bed off California, and the old man was rich all over again. The first well came in when he was sixty-one. He was living in LA. Of course, I knew all about him. He was one of the grand old men of American business, and I was fascinated by him.

One day, I got a call from a movie executive who had taken a job with Hammer. He had decided to make movies, mostly about himself. The executive asked if I wanted to help produce a TV special about Dr. Hammer's upcoming cultural tour of the Soviet Union. For me it was less an opportunity to make a television show than a chance to meet and work with and learn from one of the great *machers*. No matter your age, you never stop looking for teachers. "No," I said, "I'm not interested in a one-time project with Armand Hammer, but I might consider an exclusive deal to cover all such cultural exchanges."

Five minutes later, the phone rang. It was Hammer. He said, "Hey, kid, get over here, let's talk."

I went to meet Hammer at his office in Beverly Hills. He was a small and steely man, with a helmet of silver hair and horn-rimmed glasses. There was mischief in his eyes. He said he wanted to be where the action was. He was always in jump position. In him, I saw big deals and fun. In me, he saw himself as a kid. We had the same sensibility, we rhymed. So we called our lawyer—we had the *same* lawyer—and told him to draft an agreement. Just like that, we were partners.

I loved to listen to him talk. My stories were about the Bronx, the Air Force, Elvis, the Colonel, Zeppelin, Sinatra. His were about the Communist Party, Trotsky, Lenin, Brezhnev, Moscow in January, Nixon, and Reagan. We hatched plans, crazy ideas.

I remember a trip we made to China. There must have been

a reason for this trip, but in truth Hammer just liked to *go* for the sake of going. Airports, cities, languages—that was his thing. We spent the night on the plane, engines humming, the world black outside the window. Then Beijing came into view, a sea of lights. We were met on the tarmac by bands and diplomats. Armand was the main event wherever he happened to be. The Chinese had a manifest. It listed the dozens of people in our group. Because I was Armand's partner—in America we were Weintraub-Hammer, in the rest of the world we were Hammer-Weintraub—my name was second on the list, which, as far as the Chinese were concerned, made me something like a vice president.

Though we had been up for hours, we had no time to rest or shower and were instead hurried by motorcade to a dinner at the people's palace. This was the 1980s, not long after Nixon opened China to the West. There was still something mysterious and exotic about the country, the squat buildings and shrines, the sea of faces, the narrow lanes. It was as if we had passed through the looking glass. The party was held in the Great Hall of the People in Beijing, where we sat around an enormous table. Hundreds of waiters were coming and going. Ritual governed the slightest gesture.

Hammer occupied the seat of honor, between the premier of the nation and the chairman of the country. I was second in importance, also seated between high officials. There was a lot of eating, talking, drinking. This was followed by the toasts. They came one after another, as dignitary after dignitary raised his glass and spoke about the generosity of Dr. Hammer. At one point, I leaned over and looked at Armand to see how he was taking all this. His chin rested on his chest and his horn-rimmed glasses had slid down nose. He was asleep.

Then a little man at the end of the table raised a glass and said, "And now, we honor our other fine and honorable guest, Hollywood movie man and maker of the great film *E.T.*, Mr. Jerry Weintraub. Everyone applauded. Then the little man said, "Now Mr. Jerry Weintraub, please to stand and say a few words."

I stood, blushing, nodding through the applause. I tried to say no, no, I did not make *E.T.*, but everyone seemed so happy with me, it felt wrong to disappoint them. In the end, I gave in and signed all their stills from *E.T.*

We spent the rest of the trip in meetings with officials. Hammer, having finally gotten some sleep, was exploding with energy, shaking hands, talking, making deals, which, to him, was the same as making friends.

Hammer was unpredictable and fun. As I said, he wanted to be where the action was. I'll give you an example. During Jimmy Carter's presidency, George H. W. Bush scheduled a reception for Deng Xiaoping, a member of China's ruling Politburo, in the course of his first visit to the United States. It was a big deal. Deng Xiaoping made only three stops when he was in the country. He went to Washington for a state dinner at the White House, he went to California to visit Disneyland, he went to Texas for a dinner with George Bush. The Chinese loved Bush—he had been the American representative in the formative years after Nixon's first visit—and they wanted to let the world know how much they valued George Bush, and how important he was. Ronald Reagan took notice of the dinner, and, in my opinion, it was a factor a few years later when Reagan picked George Bush to be his running mate. The dinner would be held in Houston, Bush's hometown. Bush told me about the dinner and asked if I wanted to invite anyone and so forth.

As soon as Hammer heard about this the calls started. He

had tried to get on the list for the state dinner, but was rejected by the State Department. There were several reasons, chief among them his long relationship with the Russians. We were, after all, trying to take advantage of the rivalry between the Russians and the Chinese. After the White House turned him down, Hammer focused on the dinner in Houston. He had to be there.

But it was a no go, I couldn't do it, and Hammer finally gave up. Or so I thought. Then the night came. And Hammer showed up. No invitation? So what? There he was. I'm not sure how he got there, and do not remember the whole backstory, but Bush, who had known Hammer for years and was at that time a private citizen, said something like, "Of course, of course, he's here, let him in."

Bush introduced Hammer to Deng Xiaoping, who was thrilled to meet Hammer because he had known Lenin—so thrilled, in fact, that he insisted on being seated next to Hammer at the dinner. Everyone was sent scrambling. All the seats had to be rearranged. Hammer ended up next to Deng Xiaoping, and that's how the two of us got an invitation to visit Beijing at a time when private citizens didn't do so. And we went on a private jet, which was the only way Hammer, who was over eighty by then, would travel.

A few years later, I threw two parties at my house for Yitzhak Shamir because I really admired him. He was then prime minister of Israel. Shamir was a tough guy and a real hero. Hammer was at both parties, helping Shamir hit up the people at the dinners—forty heavyweights from LA—for money. He wanted us to drill for oil in Israel. I remember him sitting with his map, pointing to all the known fields in the region, saying, "Look, where we're sitting, there's got to be oil!" We had done surveys, tests, studies. We knew there was no oil, but he refused to believe us. He kept saying, "Gentleman, please, please, look where we're sitting! There's got to be oil."

Shamir was smart. He knew that in order to get to us, he had to get to Hammer, and to get to Hammer, he need only play on his vanity. So, at the end of dinner, the prime minister stood and said, "I would like to thank Dr. Hammer, who loves and understands Israel and is therefore going to help us drill for that oil that's just got to be there. I mean, look where we're sitting!"

Hammer, never shy of a spotlight, then said, "Uh, yes, Mr. Prime Minister. We will drill and the Jewish state will have its oil!"

Hammer went to each of us later, saying, "One million from you, one million from you, one million from you, and we find that oil."

When he came to me, I said, "Hey, Armand, I know a better way to get oil."

"What's that, wise guy?"

"Let's just sink a bit into the Saudi Pipeline."

I kicked in the money, though. It was always that way with Hammer. He was a very good salesman. (They never did find oil in Israel.)

Hammer became even more active as he got older. He wanted to go everywhere and see everything. His bags were packed, his plane was fueled, he was ready to travel with a change in the news. In the summer of 1982, while we were in the air on our way to South Korea, we got word that Leonid Brezhnev, the Russian premier, had died.

"Turn it around," Hammer told his pilot. "We're going to Moscow."

The pilot leaned on the stick, the plane banked steeply.

"What are you talking about?" I asked.

"We've got to be at that funeral," said Hammer. "It's where the action is!"

"I can't just go to Moscow like this," I said. "I don't have the clothes for it, for one thing."

"Look, Jerry," said Hammer, "history is not asking your permission. It's telling you. A man has died."

"Brezhnev was anti-Semitic," I said. "And I don't need to see him buried."

"He's been my friend forever," said Hammer. "I've got to be there."

"Fine," I said. "But I'm not going to the funeral."

"Don't worry," said Hammer. "I couldn't get you a ticket anyway."

We landed in Paris, where we were met by Soviet pilots, who flew Hammer's plane into Moscow. In those days, they did not let private jets fly into Russia, unless they were flown by Soviet pilots. I saw the vice president's plane on the runway in Moscow, *Air Force Two*, with the government crest on its side. "Look," said Hammer, "your friend is in town."

Hammer took a car to his apartment—he had houses and apartments all over the world—and I checked into a hotel. I called the U.S. Embassy and asked to talk to the vice president. Within a few seconds, Bush was on the phone. "What the heck are you doing here, Jerry?" he asked.

"I came with Armand," I said. "He came for the funeral."

"Are you going to the funeral?" asked Bush.

"No," I said. "Armand can't get me a ticket."

"I'm sorry, Jerry, I can't get you a ticket either," said Bush. "The Russians only gave us five, and I have Barbara with me, George Shultz and his wife, and Arthur Hartman, the ambassador. We don't even have a seat for his wife!"

"Don't worry," I told Bush. "I don't even want to go. Hammer dragged me here."

"I will call you when it's over," said Bush. "We'll have lunch at the Embassy."

"Great."

I hung up.

A minute later, the phone rang. It was Hammer. "Get dressed," he said, "I got you a ticket. We're going to the funeral."

It was a cold, bleak day. I got dressed and went down. Hammer was waiting with a car. We drove. The streets were gray cinder block after gray cinder block, same color as the sky. The people on the street looked gray, too. The Kremlin was surrounded by tanks and soldiers. When the car stopped, Hammer popped out as if he were on springs, handed me my ticket, and raced ahead. There was a checkpoint. When Armand went through, the soldiers saluted. When it was my turn, they started to talk in Russian, guns were pointed at me. I had a ticket, but it said "Florence Hammer"—Armand's wife. That is what set off the guards. I started shouting, "Armand! Armand!" It took a moment for him to hear me, to recognize his own name—he was getting old. Then he came back, pushed his way through, started talking to these guys in Russian. They calmed down as soon as they saw him, lowered their guns, apologized—not to me, to Armand.

We looked for our seats. It was like a Yankees game, when you keep getting closer and closer to the field and wonder, *Jeez, who does this guy know, how good are these tickets going to be?* We were on the carpet, a dozen feet from the casket, sitting with Castro, Qaddafi, and Arafat, all my favorites. The Politburo marched past me, the generals and the Red Army band. I was on all the broadcasts. As I scanned the crowd, bored, looking for familiar faces, I spotted Bush and Shultz and the rest in back, hands in their pockets, pinched by the cold and the indignity of bad seats. (The Russians did not want them to be shown on TV, so they stuck them far away from the cameras.) When I spoke to Bush later, he seemed genuinely amused. "What happened?" he said, laughing. "First I hear you're not going, then I see you, not only at the funeral but basically seated inside the coffin."

What a day! It was like stumbling into a history book. After the service, a Russian big shot came over and said, "Dr. Hammer, we want you and Mr. Weintraub to please come with us to the tomb to say good-bye to the premier before we put him in the wall."

We were taken to the wall of the Kremlin, where they buried the big shots. The world press was there. In front, it was just me, Hammer, a few Russians, and the casket. The Russians took hundreds of pictures of Hammer and me posed with the box. Each time, before the flash went off, Hammer broke into a big smile. It was his instinct. Don't let the cameras catch you looking morose! I finally said, "Hey, Armand, did you forget? Your friend died."

People age in different ways. Some go on and on, while others drop off the table. One day they are a hundred percent themselves, the next day, even if their body is still walking, a crucial piece is gone. Armand progressed like a western sunset, each moment deepening the beauty that had only been suggested in the afternoon. His pace quickened, as if he wanted to get as much as possible done, as if he wanted to finish strong. We took one of our last trips in 1984, to the Olympics in Sarajevo. We had no plans to go. Like much else with Armand, the decision was made all of a sudden, and for no reason at all. He just wanted to travel, see, experience.

"You can't just go to the Olympics," I told him. "There are no tickets, no hotels. People have been planning this trip for three years."

"Pack your bags," he said. "We're going to Sarajevo. That's where the action is."

"When do you want to go?" I asked.

"Now," he said. "Meet me at the plane."

He owned a 727, with the cabin divided into two two-bedroom suites. I used to bring a few bottles of Chateau Lafite and a bucket of Kentucky Fried Chicken. Armand loved that. He had a chef on the plane, but on most of our trips all he did was put the chicken on plates and pour the wine.

It took forever to reach Sarajevo. Hammer was eighty-four years old. The trip exhausted him. He had made no plans, no reservations, nothing. Instead, when we were an hour out, he called the president of Yugoslavia and said, "We need rooms."

"Don't worry, Dr. Hammer," said the president. "I'll take care of it."

Hammer had convinced the president that he, Hammer, would dig for coal and drill for oil, so the president would do just about anything to make him happy.

We were met at the airport by a parade of limousines and police cars, which took us to Tito's ski chalet in the mountains. (Tito had died a few years before, but his name was still spoken with great reverence.) The road climbed in switchbacks, each turn opening on a monster view of dark hills and yellow lights. It felt like we were going to the top of the world. The chalet was a palace, hundreds of rooms and galleries. We unpacked. A banquet had been arranged to honor Dr. Hammer. Now bear in mind, it was one o'clock in the morning. We were wiped out, sitting at this long table as they brought out the food—stag, grouse, a wild grub-eating boar with an apple in its mouth, the last thing in the world a Jew wants to see. They cut into its flank, shaved off strips of belly meat, fat pooling and glistening on the plate. Everybody was passing around fizzy, pale beer, making toasts, and Armand had his chin on his chest, head down.

"Do you want I should wake him?" one of the diplomats asked me.

"Nah," I said. "Let the man rest."

We finally went up to bed. I got under the covers, closed my eyes, started to doze, an American Jew surrounded by black, Slavic peaks. Then, just as I started to dream, there was a vicious banging on my door. It was scary as hell, coming in the dead of night, like a summons by the Gestapo: Send out the Juden! I sat up in bed, confused, wondering: *Who am I? Why am I here?*

"Yeah, who the hell is it?" I asked.

"It's Armand. Get packed. We're moving."

I went downstairs. There was a guard of fifty soldiers watching us, each man armed to the teeth. "There's a storm blowing in," Armand explained. "If we don't get out now, we'll be stuck here and miss the opening ceremonies of the Olympics. We can't miss the opening ceremonies. That's where the action is."

We drove back through the passes, the storm closing in behind us.

Armand was on the phone the entire way. He called every hotel in the city but could not find a room, so he called the president, got him out of bed. "We need help," said Armand. "We don't know where we're going." A palace was found in the middle of the city. It was filled with diplomats. It was completely packed, but no problem. The president kicked everyone out, ambassadors and diplomats were awakened in the dead of night and told to pack. I saw them in the halls, one shoe on, shirtsleeves hanging out of suitcases. I was given a suite of rooms on a high floor. I could see distant blue mountains over the red rooftops of the city. My living room was a ballroom, the bathroom was bigger than my house in LA. It was a fairy tale.

The next day, at the opening ceremonies, we sat with the president. It was like every other trip I'd taken with Hammer: going to be going, big wheels and diplomats, sleeping through banquets and toasts. We attended the opening ceremonies of the Games, went to some of the contests. Well, I assume we did. I don't really remember. With Armand, the event was always less interesting than the show. He wanted to be in the action, to see and be seen. He made a study of human drama—it was his life's work. He was fascinated by everyone, high and low. He wanted to find out everything. He had a special interest in charisma and power, in great men, the special few who worked their will on history. Hammer participated, but he also observed. In this, he exhibited a kind of active detachment. He was in the game but removed from the game, playing and watching himself play. He made a spectacle of himself but enjoyed watching that spectacle. He did that his entire life, until he was sick and old.

He died of bone cancer. It was very painful, but it was not the pain that bothered him. It was being stuck in a hospital bed, removed from the game. *Look at this joint! This ain't where the action is!* But I did not agree. To me, *Hammer* was the action.

He carried his own gravity—the definition of a great man. He died in 1990. When I think of him now, it is not the sick man I see but the immeasurably pleased man at the funeral in Moscow, grinning in pictures standing next to a casket. "What are you smiling for? Did you forget? Your friend died." But maybe Armand had it right. As long as you're here, you might as well smile.

The Peanut Farmer

P eople think that Hollywood and politics operate in different spheres—they don't. The world is very small at the top, with a few thousand players running everything. For a producer, an actor, a banker, a politician—name your celebrity—crossing genres is less a matter of making connections with the leaders of other industries than of climbing high enough in your own to reach the place where all lines converge. As I said, people describe me as a Republican powerbroker, a right-winger in the land of liberals, but that's not true. I am, in fact, a person who values friendship over politics, and I happen to have a lot of friends, which means I happen to have a lot of politics. As Hammer was friendly with both Lenin and Reagan, I am friendly with both Clooney and Bush.

If you were a Jew in New York when I grew up, you were a Democrat. Franklin Roosevelt was like a great-uncle to us, a benign presence who towered over everything. By watching him, you learned about power and prestige. He taught you that politics is more than conventions and elections, more than smoky backrooms. It's the neighborhood. It's life. It was Roosevelt who led the country through the Depression. It was

Roosevelt who took on the Nazis. When he was riding high, we were all riding high. When he was licked, we were all licked. I consider Franklin Roosevelt the ideal leader, the president against whom all others are measured.

Of course, all of this was in the background; it was the world of adults. Politics did not become real to me until the late fifties, and then only because of a particular incident. I was working as a record plugger, traveling the Midwest and South to promote artists. Going into a radio station in Omaha, Nebraska, I bumped into a young man coming out. This was John Kennedy, then a freshman senator. (You can say I crashed into politics.) We fell into conversation in the way of northeasterners happening upon each other far from home, and formed an instant bond. He had finished his interview and was at a loose end. So he waited for me. We went around the corner and sat down for coffee. I fell in love with him. It took sixty seconds. The charisma came off him like shimmers come off a hot road. We had a picture taken together, standing side by side in the sun. I was added to the list of people who could be contacted, counted on. I later worked for him in the presidential election, making calls, getting out the vote. I was an advance man.

From Kennedy I learned that the best politicians are not different from movie stars. They charm, communicate, command. The good ones never make you feel isolated or small, as if they have something you don't. Quite the opposite. They include you in their world, enlarge you, make you recognize the best qualities in yourself. I saw this most powerfully with Ronald Reagan. George Bush had taken me to the Alfalfa dinner in Washington. At one point, I realized that everyone in the room had been on the cover of *Time* magazine. Secretaries of state, presidents, vice presidents. But when Reagan came in, everything stopped, everyone stared, then they rushed to him like moths to a flame. Whatever moment he was in became *his* moment. Whatever room he entered became his room. Some people have that. It's the intangible quality that sells tickets and pulls nations out of funks. It's where politics becomes showbiz, and showbiz becomes transcendent. A movie or piece of art can save your life in the same way your life can be saved by a policy or law. This is why politicians seek out movie stars, and why movie stars want to become politicians. They seek the same target, which is the soul of the people.

I've worked for many public figures over the years, for mayors and congressmen, and selectmen who wanted to become mayors. I've given money and advice, hosted fund-raisers and campaigned. Contributing money and resources is my honor and responsibility as a citizen of the greatest nation on earth. (I am, for example, very proud of my work with Not On Our Watch, which battles genocide in Darfur, and which was founded by George Clooney, Matt Damon, Brad Pitt, Don Cheadle, and myself.)

The most liberal politician I've ever worked for was probably Jimmy Carter. He sought me out, reaching me through a friend. This was 1974, even before he won the Democratic presidential nomination. He was just a peanut farmer from Georgia, a nobody really, just a governor, a long shot. I could give you a big, mumbo-jumbo reason why I did not want to support him, but the simple fact is, I did not think he would win. I bet horses that figure to finish in the money. As Dino said, "Don't be a sucker." But Lew Wasserman loved Carter. Just loved the guy. *Honest. True. Integrity.* All that. He called me and said, "Listen, Jerry, Jimmy Carter is going to be president of the United States. I want you to meet him."

I fought, resisted, dragged my feet. I finally agreed to do a little work for the campaign, just to get Lew off my back, and hosted a ten-thousand-dollar-a-plate dinner for Carter. Carter and I were supposed to meet at the Century Plaza Hotel in West Hollywood for lunch, where we would really talk. But I broke the date at the last minute. I told his people I had pinched a nerve in my neck, and it was simply too painful for me to leave the house. Well, a few months go by and what happens? The peanut farmer is elected president. I get a call. *President-elect Carter wants you to meet him in Plains, Georgia.* I took my son and daughter along—he was a little kid; she was a newborn. We landed on a strip about thirty miles from the Carter farm. I stared out the window as we drove. We went through endless rows of green crops streaming past the window. We finally get to Plains. The Carters were doing that southern hospitality thing. Yes ma'am and no sir and lemonade and whatnot—the kindness that can kill you. My children were taken into the yard to play, and a secret service agent brought me in to see Carter. As I was walking in, Cyrus Vance—the next secretary of state—was walking out.

President Carter was wearing work boots with his blue jeans tucked inside. He looked like Abraham Lincoln or something. We sat down. Rosalyn brought us coffee. "How is that pinched nerve in your neck?" he asked.

"I never really had a pinched nerve," I told him.

"I know that," he said. "But why didn't you want to have lunch with me?"

"Because I didn't think you were going to become president," I said.

"Well, I am president," he said.

"Yes," I said, "I can see that."

He wanted my help in Hollywood, gathering people, getting them on board with his programs. This was outreach. I became very friendly with him. His son Chip used to stay at our house when he visited California. I liked him. I liked the president, too. Then, about six months into his presidency, he invited me to a White House state dinner for Tito. It was a hot ticket. The dictator had never been to America before. Only 110 people are invited to these dinners, so it was an honor. But I could not go. I called the State Department and asked if they could do me a favor and invite my parents instead. They said, "We're sorry, Mr. Weintraub, we just can't. This is a big dinner. We have the Supreme Court justices and senators coming. The world wants to be at this dinner. We'll invite your parents to the next one."

"Okay. Good."

A few months later, my father and mother did indeed get an invitation from the White House. It was for a state dinner honoring the president of Austria, which made sense, as my father's family originally came from Austria. I had told my father none of this, so he was naturally puzzled by the invitation. After talking to my brother, he finally decided, "You know, I bet Jerry has something to do with this."

He called me and asked, "Jerry, if I go to this thing, do I sit next to your mother at dinner?"

"No," I said. "They separate everyone. It makes for better mixing."

"Mixing," he said. "Mixing I don't need. I am not going if I can't sit with your mother. I mean, what's the point if we can't be together?"

"All right," I said. "Let me make a phone call."

I talked to the people at the State Department. It went against protocol, but I got them to seat my parents next to each other.

Before the dinner, they went though the receiving line to meet the president and first lady. As my father walked up, a man whispered in Rosalyn Carter's ear: "Sam and Rose Weintraub—Jerry Weintraub's parents."

The first lady gave them a tremendous welcome. "Oh, my golly, it's so good to meet you. Your son is one of our favorite people. Our son Chip is with him right now in Beverly Hills. Isn't that funny? He's with our son, and we're with his parents."

She called to the president, saying, "Jimmy, look, these wonderful people are Jerry's mother and father!"

Jimmy Carter said to my father, "Oh, we like your son, he's such a nice guy."

After the dinner, my parents were taken home in a town car. Along the way, my father, spotting a pay phone, asked the driver to pull over. He got out and called my brother—not me, but Melvyn!—and said, "You are not going to believe this, but your brother really does know the president."

Dancing with the Rebbe

O ne day, years ago, when I arrived at work, I spotted a
Hasidic Jew in the hall outside my office. These are
the guys in the black coats with side curls and beards. This particular rabbi was a Lubavitcher, part of the group from Crown
Heights, Brooklyn, who believe their rabbi, Menacham Mendel
Schneerson, might be the Messiah. The followers of the Rebbe
are devout. Rather than merely study and pray, they want to
heal the world, do good work, invest even the smallest errand
with a kind of godliness. I don't know all the particulars, but
it's hardcore Hebrew, whiskey straight from the jug, no mix-
ers, no water, radically different from my own casual American
Judaism, which is practiced in a synagogue designed by modern
architects.

I ducked in a side door unseen, walked into my office, got
behind my desk, went to work. My secretary came in with the
call sheet. As I looked it over, she said, "Do you know there's a
rabbi outside waiting to see you?"

"Yes," I said. "I'm aware."

"Well," she asked, "do you want to talk to him?"

"No," I said, "I don't."

"What should I tell him?" she asked.

"Here," I said. "Hand me a pen."

I wrote out a check for ten thousand dollars.

"Give him this," I said. "Tell him I'm too busy to talk, but take the money and good luck."

I would gladly have paid ten grand just to avoid one of those maddeningly circular discussions you have with rabbis.

A few minutes later, my secretary came back. "He said he doesn't want the check," she told me.

"He doesn't want the check?"

"No," she said. "He needs to talk to you, and claims it has nothing to do with money."

Now I was interested, genuinely curious. I mean, those guys never turn down a check! "All right," I said. "Send him in."

He came in and sat down. I got a look at him. I had only noticed his clothes, but now I could see that his face was intelligent and warm. (This, as I then learned, was Schlomo Cunin, who is still my rabbi.) It tells you about judging from a distance, based on generalities. I mean, there are the clothes, then there is the face; there is the face, then there is the brain; there is the brain, then there is the soul. He had a good soul. We're friends to this day. He brings me a fresh challah every week.

"What's going on?" I asked. "You don't want my check?"

"I don't need the check," he said. "I need help. I've got a problem. The check won't fix my problem."

"What's your problem?"

"I owe eight million dollars."

"You owe what?" I said. "If you think I'm going to give you eight million dollars, you're crazy."

"We don't want money," he said. "We want you to help us solve our problems."

"What do you mean, 'We'?" Who sent you here?"

"The Rebbe."

"Who's the Rebbe?"

"Menacham Mendel Schneerson. The Hasid. The leader of the Lubavitchers. He said, 'Go see this Weintraub. He is going to help us. He is going to do the work of God.'"

I sat there, dumbstruck. I looked into my coffee cup. Half full. I looked out the window. The streets were swollen with morning traffic. "It's too early for this," I said. "I'm not going to do what you want me to do, whatever that is. Just take the check and go."

He left without the check.

Time passed. Hammer and I were planning a trip. A few days before we left, I got a call from George Bush. He was then vice president. He wanted to talk. We met for lunch.

"I understand you and your friend Armand are going to Moscow," he said.

"Yeah," I said, "we're leaving in a couple of days."

"Good," said Bush. "I want you to look up a friend of mine. His name is Demachev. He is going to be important. I think you will find him interesting."

This was in the 1980s. Thousands of Jewish refuseniks were trapped in Russia. These were critics of the regime who had spoken too volubly or too well. I had gotten a list of the names and addresses of the most prominent. I planned to visit them all. This was on my mind as I planned the trip.

I went home, packed, got into bed. We were leaving early in the morning. I turned on the TV and flipped around. I happened on a cable access channel I'd never noticed before. The picture was grainy and washed out, a synagogue seen through a stationary camera. The hall was filled with hundreds and hundreds of men in black coats and hats listening with rapt attention to a bearded man. He was speaking Yiddish, his words translated into English in subtitles on the bottom of the screen. I suddenly realized that this was the Rebbe of Crown Heights. Next I realized he was talking about me. I'm not exactly sure how I realized this. He never mentioned my name or anything like that, it was just clear. "An important trip will take place tomorrow," he said. "A Jewish businessman will travel to Russia. He plans to carry the names of refuseniks in his lapel pocket. Do not do this, sir. Do not put yourself in danger. We will take care of the refuseniks. You do your business, then come home. You are needed for more important work here."

We went to Russia. I had my meetings, met with the Russian official, spoke with the refuseniks, then flew back. When we landed at LAX, I had a pain. It was terrible. I could not stand to walk off the plane. I was rushed to the hospital. Nurses and doctors stood above me, talking, poking me with needles. I was being rushed into surgery. Then, suddenly, the Hasidic Jew who I had seen in the hall outside my office was over me.

I looked up, blinked hard, looked again. I couldn't believe it.

"Rabbi?" I asked.

He put a dollar bill in my hand and said, "The Rebbe sent me. He says everything is going to be fine. He needs you here to do God's work."

As they rolled me into the operating room, I called back, almost screaming, "Yes, Rabbi, yes! If you get me out of here, I will do God's work!"

Later, in the recovery room, I found the dollar bill folded on the side table. I thought a lot about the Rebbe, faith, God. I am not an obvious target for the Lubavitchers. I am not religious. I don't obey all the laws. I go to synagogue twice a year. Pork and lobster came into my world as soon as my grandparents left it. I am not strictly observant, but I felt an intense spiritual connection to the Rebbe. The things that happened—that cable access show, the sudden illness, the dollar bill—were unexplainable, and I did not want them explained. I treasured the mystery.

Soon after I was released from the hospital, I flew to New York to meet the Rebbe. I drove to a shul on Eastern Parkway in Crown Heights. Vivid. That's the best word I have for the scene inside. Hundreds of Hasidic Jews, a sea of black coats, rocking as they prayed, lips moving, mouths filled with the holy words, minds crowded with visions of God. There were at least a thousand people in the room. When the Rebbe came in—I was waiting for him near the Torah, as had been arranged—the people in the sanctuary, three or four thousand of them crowded in like sardines, stopped talking, praying, breathing. Every eye was on this man with a gray beard and sparkling blue eyes. The crowd opened like the Red Sea as he walked through the room.

He came near me. He was a little man, but also the biggest man I have ever seen. He was small, but he was huge. And he had a face, well, it was as close to the face of God as you are likely to see on earth. That was my sense, my dazzled, knocked-out sense. It was expressive and warm and gave off a glow. You felt wide awake in his presence, but also calm. I think that's a good way to describe it: also calm. He came up to me and took my hand, and his hand was warm. He was a brilliant man, he had attended the Sorbonne in Paris, and was a terrific writer, and spoke about a dozen languages. But he was simple, too, and earthy, all about the eternal and important, the only things that matter and last. When he spoke to me, everything was still, no one moved—I mean, these were people who jumped up and down and yelled and prayed fiercely, but not when the Rebbe was speaking. I do not remember everything he said, but the particulars were less important than the general sense, the impression he gave—that he was here and I was here and no one has to be alone. Then we stood side by side and read from the Torah.

The Rebbe comforted me about life and death. He made me see that my general, uneducated sense of the world—that there is a God, an order, a plan—was not superstition or error, but correct, built into me for a reason, as my heart or lungs are built into me. Without it, I could not live. Which is why you need more than material things. I mean, yes, the material can be nice. I like having what I have, but I know none of it is mine, that we are only renters on earth, that even our bodies belong to someone else. Which is why you hunger even when you've had your fill. Life will never satisfy if it is experienced only as the rise and fall of commerce. You need to see yourself as part of something larger that never dies.

When I left that day, I was a different person.

I brought my father and brother to meet the Rebbe. I had been talking a lot about my experience, and my father was giving me that skeptical look of his. "So, Jerry, tell me, how does your friend the Rebbe think we should proceed?" The coats and hats, the beards—it was not his thing. We went in the afternoon. My father was not doing well. He was having trouble with his back and was bent over in pain. I helped him up to the altar. The Rebbe reached out and took his hand. I looked at my father's face. He was transfixed, transfigured. He and the Rebbe were locked in a moment. Something was happening. It was beyond me—it was just between them. I didn't understand it. When we left the shul, my father was standing straight, without pain. I'm not talking about a Rex Humbard laying on of hands, or Oral

Roberts healing on TV. I'm talking about something subtle and real—about a man who can lift you up and change your mind. We went in crooked, but came out straight.

I started helping the Lubavitchers, doing what I promised to do as I was wheeled into surgery. It began thirty years ago, when neo-Nazis burned down the Chabad house in Westwood. To raise the money to rebuild—because the best answer is a new shul—I decided to do one thing I knew I was good at: put on a show. It was their idea, but I knew how to put it together. We've staged a Chabad telethon every year since, raising millions of dollars, with appearances by, among others, Bob Dylan. The telethon has earned a cult following. Groups of comedians gather in living rooms each fall to watch me dance with the rabbis. I raise my hands and kick my feet, feeling in no way self-conscious or embarrassed. I might be dancing in front of the cameras, but I am dancing with the Rebbe.

The Rebbe left this earth in 1994. Thousands of worshippers filled Eastern Parkway in Brooklyn and mourned. Who was this man, the same as the rest of us, but entirely different? Was he a prophet, was he the Messiah, was he a Hasid? I don't know, and I don't think anyone else knows, either. I don't think it's our business to know. I do think he was as godly as any man who ever lived. And I know what he gave to me when he was here, that tremendous sense of peace and solace, and what he gives me still, even though he is gone. When I am troubled, I talk to him, and his face is there.

If You Find Something You Love, Keep Doing It

Every small man wants to be a big man, every big man wants to be a king. It's human nature. By the eighties, having achieved many of my goals, I began to dream the dream of all producers—total control. I wanted to cross the lot in the manner of Zanuck. I wanted to sit in the big seat and make the wheels go round. I wanted to run a studio. It started in 1984, when Kirk Kerkorian, the industrialist and one of the wealthiest men in LA, purchased United Artists, a studio that traced its lineage to Charlie Chaplin, Mary Pickford, and Douglas Fairbanks, its founders. The studio had fallen on hard times and Kerkorian said I was the man who could fix it. I was named to head United Artists that summer.

It was not an easy decision for me. It meant joining the establishment, going legit. I was the rough rider who dons the badge to clean up the town, for what is an independent producer if not a kind of cowboy, out on his own? In the end, though, it seemed like an opportunity I could not pass up. By this time, I had made every kind of movie and every kind of hit. I was ready for something new. The problem was not my decision. It was my boss: Kirk Kerkorian. Simply put, we had the same dream: total control. As I hired staff and began planning projects, I realized he had given me the title but not the job. A title without a job is the worst of all worlds: it means taking all the blame while getting none of the credit and having none of the fun. I began to plan my exit soon after I arrived.

Due to my contract, I left United Artists with a tremendous severance. I had invested thirty million dollars, but I left with a lot more. This became the story, as it made me look like a genius. Jerry Weintraub worked at United Artists for less than three months and walked off with tens of millions. It was portrayed as a master move, as if I had taken the job with the sole intention of getting out with all I could carry. As usual, the reporters missed the real story, which was my terrible sense of failure and lost opportunity. I was heartbroken. It was not money that I wanted—I had lots of money—it was the chance to run a studio. And, in fact, the little taste I did have made me crave the challenge even more. It became an obsession.

In 1985, I formed my own film company, the Weintraub Entertainment Group. I first went about raising money, because what is a trip to Vegas without a bankroll? In other words, you need to spend money to make money, and I wanted to start with the biggest roll in town. The dream of building your own movie studio is an old dream. The path is piled with corpses. One reason is financing. If you don't have enough money to start with, you do not have enough money to fail. Two or three clunkers will put you out of business. I wanted to be able to weather a long dry spell—only then, I figured, would I have time to reach critical mass, the point at which a business becomes self-sustaining. I raised some money and put in some more of my own.

I rented offices in West Hollywood. The rooms had floor-to-ceiling windows through which you could see hills and cars moving in the canyons. There was art on the walls, shag on the floors, Perrier in the refrigerators, no expense spared. People judge on first sight, so make those surfaces shine. If you want to be seen as a major, look like a major. As a great man said, perception is reality. As another great man said, You grow into the suit. As a philosophy this means operating on confidence, in the belief that something will happen, that the trick will work, that the backup will arrive with the heavy guns. It's how America has operated from the beginning.

I hired a staff, recruiting talent from studios and agencies all over town. What these people had in common was a belief that we could accomplish what had not been accomplished in a generation—the creation of a new factory. These were, for the most part, established executives, men and women with families and careers behind them, meaning they were experienced and knowledgeable, and also meaning they were expensive. I suddenly found myself mired in a sea of health plans and pension benefits. In this way, we accrued a great mountain of debt before the first writer was contracted or the first scene was filmed. If I had known what to look for, I would have seen it in the early balance sheets—money going out (left pocket) versus money coming in (right pocket)—a terrible premonition

The company existed for less than four years. In this time, we made a handful of movies—these were distributed by Columbia Pictures—including *Fresh Horses*, *The Big Blue*, and *My Stepmother Is an Alien*. I promoted these films every way I knew how—George Bush, then president, was at the premiere of *My Stepmother Is an Alien*, generating a shower of publicity. But the trouble was evident early on. What makes a major a major is its ability to float a sea of debt. This is needed less to make movies than to weather flops. You need enough not merely to survive one dud, but to survive a season of duds, a worst-case scenario not at all infrequent in the business. In the case of a small studio, even one that has been well financed, the margin of error shrinks. With each flop, debt accrues and pressure grows. Each new movie is more important than the last. As the stakes increase, so does the fear, until the mood in the office and on the sets becomes intolerable, exactly the wrong atmosphere in which to make a movie. There was bickering and second-guessing; some people quit, others were fired. Part of it had to do with bad luck—a movie opened at the wrong time, it rained that weekend, and so forth—part of it had to do with bad planning. If I had known two years would go by without a hit, I might have made fewer films—but most of the problems resulted from a basic flaw: The movies were not very good.

This, in turn, resulted from a still more fundamental error, a flaw in the very conception of the business: I loved making movies, which resulted in hits, which increased my love, which sparked a desire for control, which caused me to start my own studio, which—and here is the paradox—took me out of the movie business and put me into the company running business, occupied not with writers and artists, but with health-care plans, office rivalries, and infighting. I had, in a sense, promoted myself right out of the job I always wanted, which was telling stories, producing. I lost touch with the films, which were now being made *for* me instead of *by* me and thus were no longer Jerry Weintraub Productions.

Of course, if the movies had been good, if they had drawn audiences, if they'd had kids doing the crane kick in the parking lot, everything else would have taken care of itself. But the movies were not good. I realized this little by little, then in a great rush. Success had caused me to cease doing what made me successful. More important, it had caused me to stop doing what I loved. I recall this period reluctantly. People say you learn more from failure than success; it's true. From this period, which runs like a ridgeline between my middle years and my true adulthood, I learned the great lesson of business: If you find something you love, keep doing it.

A business fails like a levee or a body fails. Everything is okay until it's not. There is a break, a wall caves in, the flood rushes through. For us, this meant debts we could not repay, movies we could not finish, bonds we could not redeem. I take full responsibility for this. It was all my fault. Did I feel sorry for myself? You bet. I was drowning in self-pity. It felt like I was watching this beautiful edifice I had constructed over the course of a career wash away at the first high tide. The banks were involved, the creditors were involved, the government was involved. When it was over, the company was gone. I was fifty years old. I had lost $30 million.

When the pressure was too great, I got on a plane and went to Florida. I wanted to be out on the water, the horizon ringed by water, the sun on the water and a line taut with a big fish. My mind was reeling. I did not know what to do, or where I would go next.

Luckily for me, I had a father, and he was a piece of steel. I went to see him. I was in tears, a grown man crying real tears. I said, "Oh, Pop, you got to help me. Look what happened. Look how hard I have fallen. Look how much I lost. I have troubles, real troubles. I've made such a failure, Pop, such a terrible failure."

Here's what he said: "You've got troubles, kid? Real troubles? Well, I tell you what. Put your troubles in a sack. Bring them to the end of the road, where you will find a lady in a store filled with sacks. She will take your sack of troubles and, in return, let you leave with any sack you want."

In the end, I was saved by my friends, all the people I had known and worked with over the years. Barry Diller, Michael Eisner, Steve Ross, Bob Daly, who was the co-CEO of Warner Bros., Terry Semel, Sid Sheinberg, who was the chief operating officer of MCA, Lew Wasserman, the people who ran the studios, they all backed me up and supported me. It was not just that they offered me jobs and opportunities, which they did, but that they showed confidence in me, and were certain I would make it all the way back. I especially remember a conversation I had with Steve Ross, who was the CEO of Warner Communications. "What are you worrying about?" he said. "You are a talented guy. That talent did not go away. The company went away? So what! Companies always go away. They're a dime a dozen. It's talent that counts!"

I was soon back in business, working from a bungalow on the lot at Warner's, where I had signed a contract to make movies. I don't care if you get flattened a thousand times. As long as you get up that thousand-and-first time, you win. As Hemingway said, "You can never tell the quality of a bullfighter until that bullfighter has been gored."

Playing Myself

O nce upon a time, I went to school to be an actor, another borough boy just home from the service. Through this window, you see me on a stage, trading punches with James Caan. Through that window, you see me running out of Capezio empty-handed, the vision of me in tights hot in my mind. I thought my career in front of the cameras had come to an end before it started, but I would eventually appear in several movies, acting work becoming a subgenre in my career. I have played myself in various films, some of my own (*Vegas Vacation, Ocean's Eleven, Twelve, Thirteen*), some made by friends (*Confessions of a Dangerous Mind, Full Frontal*). I learned to act only when I learned how to be myself, which is, of course, another kind of character. In short, I learned how to act—and I am not saying I'm a good actor, only that I'm comfortable in front of a camera—after I learned how to stop acting. When Martha Graham told me to walk across the floor, I was aware that I was a kid acting like he was crossing the floor. Now that I am an old man, I can simply cross the goddamn floor without thinking too much about it.

I appeared in my first film in 1991, at the insistence of Sydney Pollack, an old friend, who was directing *The Firm*, a legal thriller based on a novel by John Grisham. (Sydney was one of the great directors, the maker of, among others, *Out of Africa, Tootsie, The Electric Horseman,* and *Absence of Malice.*) He wanted me to play Sonny Capps, a mobbed up client of the firm who, in a key scene, spars with Tom Cruise and Gene Hackman. The part seemed like a perfect fit for Sydney himself, who had done terrific turns in several films, including *Tootsie* and *Eyes Wide Shut.*

I said, "Look, Sydney, you do it. You'd be great."

"You'd be greater," he said. "Jerry, you are Sonny Capps."

"Why don't you be me being Sonny Capps," I said. "You'd be better at me being Sonny that I'd be myself. You were my teacher at the Neighborhood School. You know I'm not an actor."

Sydney laughed. He was a great friend—he died two years ago, and not a day goes by when I do not think about him. He had one of the great infectious laughs. It started in his chest and rose through his body, filling his lungs and eyes, warming everyone around him. He said, "No, Jerry, this part is written for you."

I said, "No."

He said, "Yes."

After much discussion, I finally agreed to do it. He could be persistent.

The scene was being shot in the Caribbean. I started worrying about my performance on the flight down. I mean, what the hell do I know about acting? What's worse, I was to play the scene with Gene Hackman and Tom Cruise, two of the biggest stars in the world. How was I going to do this? I was tight. I was scared. Self-confidence and pride, those were the only things getting me through.

I went to the set in a new suit, with my hair done up and

makeup on. Sydney looked over. "All right," he said. "You look good. Are you ready?"

"Hell yes, I'm ready."

He sat me in front of the cameras with Cruise and Hackman. It was a change, going in front of the cameras. It was unnerving. I felt like a soldier caught in the sights of his own army's guns. You get fame and notoriety in front of the camera, but lose everything else.

In my scene, which comes halfway through the film, I grow increasingly irritated as Hackman and Cruise, lawyers at the firm, try to sell me on a course of action. I finally snap at Cruise, who, in his response, demonstrates his mettle. We rehearsed it, then filmed it, then filmed it again and again and again. Sydney was a perfectionist. He did not want to quit until he got it just right. Sitting there, I could not help but think like a producer: How much footage have we gone through, how much money have we burned up? It was endless, and I was frustrated. These shots, one after another, all seemingly the same—it was like repeating the same word over and over. The whole thing turned into gibberish.

We finally stopped for lunch. I asked Sydney, "Well, how's it going?"

"We got a little more to do," he said.

"We can't," I told him. "I'm exhausted."

He said, "Look, Jerry, you are not a producer here. You're an actor. We go till we get it right."

I sat back down. I was tired, spent, at the end of me. Then, finally, after the who-knows-what take, Tom Cruise turned to me and said, "You know, you've got some nerve!"

"Excuse me?"

"You heard me," he said, "you've got some nerve coming onto a set with real actors, using up our energy and wasting our time."

I turned and looked at him, goddamn piece of garbage, talking to me this way. I flushed red. I could actually feel the blood running into my face. "Who the fuck do you think you're talking to?" I said. "Do you know what you're doing?"

Just then, Sydney yelled, "Cut—we got it."

I was sitting there dazed, at a loss.

Cruise started laughing. He grabbed my arm and said, "No, no, Jerry. It's not real. Sydney told me to do it for the scene. For the scene."

I looked around, then I started laughing, too. I said, "Sydney, my God, you bum!"

"It was just what I wanted," said Sydney. "Jerry being Jerry."

A Ride in the Hills

By the 1990s, my wife, Jane, and I were in different places. "I don't want to do this anymore," she said one day. "I don't want to run to all the premieres and parties. I want to paint. I want to read. I want to be with my children in my house and look at the ocean." In this way, while still loving each other deeply, Jane and I began to move in separate directions. We saw less of each other, and usually slept in different cities. It created a space, and it was in this space that the other great love of my life bloomed.

When people hear the details of my existence, they focus on the geometry of my romantic life.

Let me start at the beginning.

One morning, as I came into my office at Warner Bros., I noticed a new girl in the office, a redhead, a knockout. I waited a few minutes, then called my secretary.

"Who's the new girl?" I asked.

"Do you mean Susie?" she asked.

"With the red hair?" I said.

"Yes, she has red hair. That's Susie."

"Great," I said. "Talk to her for me. See if she knows how to ride."

"How to ride?"

"Yeah, ask if she wants to go horseback riding with me tomorrow morning."

So they called Susie and said, "Mr. Weintraub wants to take you for a horseback ride. Do you know how to ride?"

Susie said, "Sure I know how to ride."

When she got off that call, she phoned her sister and asked, "Is it hard to ride a horse?"

"No, it's easy," he sister told her, "just grab those leather things and hang on."

I met Susie at the Equestrian Center. She was beautiful, petite, with long hair and a smile that made the day. She was outfitted like a rider, in jeans and cowboy boots. I had a gorgeous horse picked out for her. It was a spirited animal, but she said she knew how to ride. As soon I saw her in the saddle, though, holding the horn with fear in her eyes, I knew she had never been on horseback in her life. I admired Susie even more for not being able to ride, for the way she took the challenge, put out her chin, and tried her best. It was like something I would do.

"Come on, Susie," I said, holding out my hand. "Let's get you on a better horse."

We found a grandma of an animal and rode into the mountains. The hills were studded with wildflowers, the meadow grass stirred, the horses whinnied as they cantered over the passes. We talked about this and that. I made jokes, some funny, some not. Susie laughed at them all. We got off the horses and walked under the trees. I made a pass, which Susie pretended to miss. Then one thing led to another, which is an oblique way of saying I fell in love.

Susie and I courted for months. I use the old-fashioned word deliberately, as there was something proper about it despite my being married. We went to dinners and to shows, on picnics and for car rides. I knew I had to tell Jane. A little dalliance here and there, okay, but this was something else, something wonderfully serious.

Jane and I talked in Malibu. This was one of the most remarkable conversations I've ever had. I told Jane everything: about how I met Susie and about how I felt. I said, "Jane, I have fallen in love with another woman."

She sat there, listening, thinking, then spoke. Did she say, "You bastard!" Did she say, "I will see you in court!"? No. Jane was in a different place in her life. She had lived as a star, she had lived as a wife, she had lived as a liberated woman and as a working woman and as a career woman and, most important, as a mother. She loves me and I love her, but her identity was never bound up with mine. She understood what had happened and why. She understood what she could give me and what I needed. When I offered her a divorce, she said, "No, I do not want a divorce."

"It's silly to get a divorce unless you really need a divorce," she explained. "It doesn't matter to me. I'm not with anybody, and I don't intend to be with anybody. I want to paint and have a quiet life. Your life is not quiet, I know that. You have a busy life and I support it and will never stop supporting it, because I love you. And I know you love me. And we have children and grandchildren. And those things are important. They're not to be thrown away. They're not to be treated like they're something that doesn't mean anything. And what will divorce give us? Contention. Aggravation. I don't want to sit with a lawyer, and go through this and that, and you shouldn't either. You worked hard for your money—do you really want to pay millions of dollars to figure out a divorce? For what? To someday, hopefully, get back to the situation we already have today, where everyone can sit in a room together at a wedding or a funeral? There is no reason for a divorce. We can work it out. If Susie doesn't need to get married to you right now, let it go. I'm fine with it."

She was so wise, so wonderful.

"What about the children?" I asked. "What about the grandchildren?"

"We will talk to the children and grandchildren," she said. "I will explain it to them. I will say, 'Look, there is no reason for animosity. I am fine with this, you should be fine with it, too. There is no reason for you not to be friendly with Susie or close to Susie.'"

And that's what we did. We sat with the children and grandchildren, and told them, and they were all right with it. We told our friends, and some could not understand and were terribly bothered about this arrangement—okay, you are not us, you don't have to live like us.

The simple fact is, Jane no longer wanted my life. She didn't want to go to parties, didn't want to have sex with me. Not interested. Good. She needs what she needs and I need what I need, which is to be with somebody who wants to be involved in every part of my life: mentally, emotionally, sexually. Warren Beatty, lothario of lotharios, once asked me the secret. "How did you make it work, Jerry? How do you pull it off?"

Well, the answer is, I didn't. Jane and Susie did. I have a life with Susie and I love Susie, but I'm still with Jane, too. I see her all the time, and we're on the phone constantly. I will be there whenever she needs me. Otherwise, I am off, in my own life. I think this works only because Jane had such a long and successful career. She was a singer, she was a star, she was a mother. She had many lifetimes without me and I have had many lifetimes without her. She never lived through me. We used to live together; now we live apart. When marriage was invented, people didn't live very long. When I was a kid, if a couple had a fiftieth wedding anniversary, they were ancient. Nowadays, with the medicine and the longevity we have, when you marry somebody, you are in it for a very, very long time. I don't know if that's the way it's supposed to be. It's not for me, anyway. I have been with Jane for forty-eight years. I'm one of the ancients now. But I am still here, which means I am still living, still changing.

I later learned that Susie descends from Hollywood royalty. Her mother's godmother was Fanny Brice. Her mother's father was an Academy Award–winning writer. Her father was Bud Ekins, the legendary stuntman. Bud always had a passion for motorcycles. Wheels, crankshafts, throttles—he could not get enough. He used to ride wide open, burning up the desert east of LA. He was a legend in the racing world. In the 1960s, he won four gold medals at the Six-Day Trials in France and England. He won or came close to winning dozens of races in America and all over the world. He was known as the desert fox, a charismatic star, cool before that attitude went mainstream, tough as hell, with a cigarette forever hanging from the corner of his mouth.

His motorcycle shop in LA—he sold Triumphs—was a haunt of leather-clad riders and wannabes, including young movie stars eager to soak up Bud's authenticity. Steve McQueen was a regular, hanging around the garage talking to Bud, who, in his greasy white T-shirt, grimaced and said, "Yeah, yeah, hand me that spring hook over there." When McQueen was shooting *The Great Escape*, he asked Bud if he would be his stuntman double. It was Bud Ekins who, on a Triumph TR6, performed the famous jump that carried Steve McQueen over a wall of concertina wire. Bud was sought out after that. He appeared in dozens of films and TV shows: racing a Mustang up and down the streets of San Francisco in *Bullitt*, running a motorcycle up the stairs of the fraternity house in *Animal House*, doubling for Ponch in the more hair-raising sequences of *Chips*.

I got an incredible kick out of Bud: the way he looked and walked, how he went at each insane stunt with a carefree ease. I want to make a movie about him, a biopic, in which he will be played by Brad Pitt, because who is the star really, the man who stood for the movie still, or the man who cleared the concertina wire?

Bud was an older man when I knew him, ailing from a life of machines, whiskey, and cigarettes. I sat with him in the hospital when he was sick. I loved the guy. He was a Catholic, so a priest went into his room, but he did not want a priest.

I asked him why.

"Why?" he said. "Because I don't want to confess all the shit I did, that's why."

He asked about rabbis. "When they come, do you have to tell them everything?"

"Nah," I said, "you don't have to tell them anything."

Soon after that he told me he wanted to convert to Judaism. "'Cause you're a Jew and Susie is a Jew," he said. (Susie converted.) "And I figure I'm whatever you guys are. Also the confession stuff."

I gave a eulogy at Bud's funeral. I spoke of how he had

decided to become a Jew. Many of the mourners looked confused. These were stuntmen and bikers, hundreds of tough guys with long hair and leather coats, giant guys named Tiny. "Let me explain why he became a Jew," I said. "Because Bud Ekins did not want to confess his sins." With that, the stuntmen and bikers went wild, hooting and cheering, a good send-off for a great man.

Farewell to Sam and Rose

No matter how old you are, everything changes when your parents die. The wall between you and death collapses; suddenly gone are the only people who could speak with true authority. My life has been spent chasing mentors, each of them being like a substitute parent, but when your real parents die, you realize certain things are irreplaceable. They go and never come back. It's a blow. This is what it means to be an orphan.

My mother got sick first. By this time, I'd been sick myself, with prostate cancer. I won't go into detail, except to say it reminded me of the fragility of life. We are all walking on a wire. The key is to behave as if you will live forever. Her first symptoms presented themselves as anxiety or forgetfulness. This was in the late 1980s. She was still my mother, still the same woman with the same face and hands, but the curtain was coming down. She was diagnosed with Alzheimer's. Each day was a little worse than the day before. She got lost in her own neighborhood, then her own house, then her own mind. She couldn't recognize friends and family. It was very hard on my father. Here was this woman, the great love of his life, sitting next to him as always, but already gone. It was obvious to me that something had to be done; the situation could not go on. My father could not make that decision because it was too painful. My brother could not do it because he was too close. Distance allowed me to see the situation more clearly. I flew to New York, went to the apartment, took my mother to the Riverdale Home for the Aged. When my father objected, I said, "This is what we're doing." It was the most painful day of my life. My father went over there every morning, did what he could, watched her fade—God knows what he was thinking.

She died on April 30, 2000. I stood at her graveside, said the prayers, and cried. A man without a mother is a man without a country, an exile. You never recover from it. My mother was the Bronx and the family and the streets at sundown and the merchants in the shops and the smoke and the smell of cooking and the train rattling over Jerome Avenue, the safety and love of family, everyone at the table, the world when the world was whole.

My father was now alone for the first time in more than fifty years. He did not talk about what was going on inside him, how he felt, any of that. That was his generation—they worked for us, gave up their lives and bodies for us, without a whisper of regret or complaint. My brother and I went on with our lives, too. It's the way with the titanic events, a death in the family, the loss of an indispensable person. The world should end, but it does not. It goes on, and carries you with it.

About eight weeks after the funeral, I was in Kennebunkport with Jane. I tend to get bored in Maine, and spend most of the time driving around. One morning, as we passed a Ford dealership, I said to Jane, "I want to buy a new car."

"Why?" she said. "You already have two other cars and a truck."

"It's an urge," I said.

We went in. They had just come out with On-Star, the service that tells you where gas stations and restaurants are, gives directions and the rest. I was impressed, saw a future in which no one gets lost and everyone eats just what they want to eat. I left with a new Ford. That night, my father called me. "What are you up to?" he asked.

"Nothing," I said. "Just hanging around."

He said, "Well, why don't you come down to New York and see me?"

"Is anything wrong?"

"No," he said. "Everything is fine. Just take a ride."

"Well, I just bought a new car," I said. "I think I will go for a ride."

Jane and I left for New York in the morning. We were on the road for two hours when my brother called and told us, "Dad is going into the hospital."

"What's wrong with him?"

"I don't know. The doctor says he's fine, but he's insisting he be admitted to the hospital."

It was strange.

We drove on, passed little towns and diners, the road stretching before us. We took a wrong turn in the Bronx and somehow ended up on the streets where I grew up. It was as if something was leading us there, showing us all the settings of my childhood—where my father taught me the value of work, where we hugged in the street after his return from Ceylon. Jane wanted to see everything, all of it. I took her to the old shops and corners. I took her to P.S. 70 and the apartment on the Grand Concourse. We knocked on the door. A woman answered. There were thirty, forty people inside. I think it was a crack house.

Everyone was at the hospital—my nephews and nieces—sitting in the hall, waiting. My brother took me aside.

"What the hell is going on?" I asked.

"I don't know," said Melvyn. "Dad wants to see us in his room alone."

He was sitting up in bed. No tubes, no wires, none of that. He waved us over, brought us close to him. He was lucid and calm. "I want you two guys to know something," he said. "You've been great sons. I love you both very, very much. And I am very proud of you. Now, both of you, give me a hug."

We bent over and hugged him. I could feel his fingers clasping my back. "Now go," he said. "I need to rest."

Later, when we were sitting in the hall, the sirens went off. The nurses and doctors ran into the room, and he died. Lay down and died.

This was June 30, 2000—exactly two months after my mother went.

When my mother was laid out before her funeral she had a pained look on her face. She had gone through hell before she passed. But my father had a peaceful look on his face when he died. He was ninety-three or ninety-four. We never really knew their exact ages. He wasn't in pain, he was just ready. That's how I'd like to die.

Until a few years ago, I was terrified of death. It occupied a lot of my time. Then my friends started to die, contemporaries, like Sydney Pollack, Bernie Brillstein, Guy McElwaine. I went to see Guy at his house, at the end, when he knew he was dying. And you know what? He was smiling.

"What are you smiling at, crazy man?" I asked.

"You," he said, "because I can see that you are afraid of

what's happening to me. But I'm not afraid, so why should you be? It's just another journey."

I thought about this again and again. It bothered me. Finally, one night, I sat down with a glass of wine and sort of interrogated myself. "What *are* you scared of?" I asked. "It's the natural progression, part of the journey. Besides, you can't get out of it. No matter how much you worry, it is going to happen. So why not just face it like you've tried to face everything else?"

The next morning, I went out and bought a cemetery plot. I have come to terms, made peace. Not because of religion, or because of anything I've been told, but because I've lost friends and I've lost family. Maybe this is what happens if you live a long life. Maybe it's the gift of survival. When more of the people who really mattered are gone than remain, the balance tilts to the next world. Your parents go, your friends go, and you realize you will go, too, and it's okay. Death makes the rope taut—without it, we would have no stories, no meaning.

I do not want to leave. I have a nice house and a nice pool and it's a beautiful day and my cellar is filled with wine and my humidor is filled with cigars. I don't want to go anywhere. But when God calls, I will go, and I won't be crying.

Oceans

Hollywood has changed. There was a golden age and an age of rebellion, and we are now in an age of post-glamour. The stars are faded, the pictures are abbreviated, and the screens are small.

Well, that's what some people tell you—that Hollywood was never the same after the old system was broken—but don't believe it. I have seen era give way to era, can compare epoch to epoch. The stars now are exactly the same as the stars then: The hot spots and clubs have changed, the styles and fashions, but the underlying motivations, the human drives, which are to be discovered and lauded and respected, never change.

Look at the young stars. They go into crazy clubs, get whacked up and whatever, but when the Macombo and Ciro's and Romanoff's were open in the forties and fifties, it was no different. The booze was flowing, Desi Arnaz was singing "Babaloo," and Joan Crawford was dancing on the tables. The media is what changed. The amount of attention, the size of the lens. In the old days, the problem could always be taken care of. The accident was followed by the phone call and the stars were back on the set in the morning. Nowadays, everything is shown on live TV.

Ocean's Eleven, *Twelve*, and *Thirteen*, which together grossed over a billion dollars, have been a capstone on my career. I did not produce the 1960 original but was around when it was made and had long wanted to do a remake; it was the perfect vehicle for young Hollywood, a way to put a handful of actors in a frame built for the original Rat Pack—to show that, though times have changed, there are still those who can shed Sinatra-size wattage. *Ocean's Eleven* screamed to be back on the marquee.

In 1998, I sent the script to Steven Soderbergh and George Clooney, who had a production deal with Warner's. We met at the Smoke House restaurant for one of those legendary meals, after which you know things will be more fun. These guys made the whole thing work. The feat of a project like this is casting, getting huge stars, Matt Damon, Brad Pitt, George Clooney, Elliott Gould, Julia Roberts, Andy Garcia, Don Cheadle to appear and mesh on the same set. Soderbergh and Clooney had everything to do with pulling this off. They contacted the actors and explained the beauty of the project—this is as close as you can get to old Sinatra days. It was important that Clooney made the calls because he got people to take less money and less back end because it was an ensemble piece. When we sent the script to Julia Roberts we attached a twenty-dollar-bill and a note that said, "We know you get twenty for a movie, but you will have to work for a little less on this one."

We had a great time making *Ocean's*. For the actors, this joy was often expressed in pranks, most of them directed at me. There was the time that, on a long flight back from Europe, Brad and George, knowing that I am a big vodka drinker, challenged me to a contest. I said, "Look, you're making a mistake. You'll end up with your luggage under your seat." They persisted, so we went shot for shot. I passed out after fifteen.

The boys then took the opportunity to fill my clothes, pockets, socks, and shoes with M&M's, thousands of them. Candy was coming out of my ears for weeks. I found out later that, as I had been downing Stolichnaya, they had been drinking water. Nice friends. Then there was the time that George Clooney, after a late night, had a huge breakfast delivered to my room at 5:00 A.M. I got so angry, but the room-service operator kept insisting that I had placed the order myself. When I finally asked where the call had come from, she said, "Matt Damon's room, but it was you calling, Mr. Weintraub."

George Clooney and all those guys can do spot-on Jerry Weintraub imitations.

All that fun we had making *Ocean's* is captured in the film. You can feel it. It's on the screen. When the movie opened in the summer of 2001, it was a smash, the biggest hit of my career. More important, it started my friendship with a group of actors, Pitt, Clooney, Damon, whom I've come to regard as family. These men are just as important to me as Sinatra and the Colonel were. I travel with them, sit with them, listen to them, love them. They are like my children. I learn from them, and I hope they learn from me, and have fun—developing true friendships, later in life, well, it's one of the great things that can happen to a person. It's like a third act when the third act works. It's a blessing. (I should also mention Bruce Willis here. He did not star in these movies, but he is a feature player in my life, a great artist and friend, another one of Jerry's kids.)

Life is strange. I used to be a kid, sitting at the feet of giants, hanging out with the last of the old-timers. Now, all of a sudden, I am the old-timer, the alter cocker who's been around forever, has known everyone and seen everything. When I look back, I see key moments. Because I did not want to go into the jewelry business. Because I would not wear tights. Because I did not want to return the messages on the call sheet. I see patterns, too. Whenever I felt the urge to obfuscate, as when Lew Wasserman asked, "Were you on the WATS line last night?" I told the truth instead. I asked if I did not know. I listened when someone else was talking. I sold with joy, so my products were fun to buy. Most important, I was never afraid to fail, which meant I was never afraid to try. I was never afraid to look silly, which meant I was never threatened by a new idea. I see the road ahead, too, a stretch that bends into the undergrowth. I do not know what will happen there, but I do know, whatever it is, I will rush to meet it with joy. This is, after all, a Jerry Weintraub Production.

ACKNOWLEDGMENTS

If there were true justice in the world, I would be saying thank you every day, from the moment I get up till the moment I lie down—that's how lucky I've been, how many great people I've known, how much goodness I've experienced. In place of that—I would like to say thanks for several years, but I have dinner reservations—I have listed some of the people who have meant the most to me:

Key Friends and Players, People So Unusual They Fit in No Category or Box; I Was Lucky to Walk the Earth at the Same Time as All of Them

Bryan Lourd: He's a friend and confidant. There has never been another agent like him. He is one of a kind, and truly important in my life and in the lives of Hollywood's biggest stars.

Bernie Yuman: We talk every day, and it's the part of the day I look forward to most. There is, in fact, not a moment when I am confused about who Bernie is—my friend, one of the best, and a man who I know loves me, and who knows I love him, dearly.

Mike Meldman: I was never interested in development until I visited Mike's golf courses—he builds the best in the world. He's a friend who makes it fun, and is the reason I am in the real estate business.

Steve Roth: This kid, this friend, this talented agent and businessman, lives around the corner, which keeps my life interesting. I want to thank him for use of his lawn—he knows what I mean.

Gerald Parsky: He saw me through the toughest time in my career, and got me away not just whole, but with a huge settlement. Thank you!

Paul Bloch: I have worked with him and admired him for more years than can be counted . . . He handles all the press and PR that I get credit for. He is one of the great ones.

Steven Soderbergh: I know he's in the book, on one of those pages where I recount some adventure, but he's been so important in my life I wanted to mention him again. And there—I just did.

Diane Sawyer: If I owned a TV station, this is who I would hire first. She is what owners in the sports world call a franchise player, an absolutely stellar talent.

Ken Ziffren: My lawyer, my confidant, my friend. Thanks for keeping me out of jail (that's a joke).

Harvey Gettleson: He can read a deal like Gretzky reads the ice: Thanks for your guidance, expertise, and friendship.

George Schlatter: George produced some of the most important shows and television events ever, many with me. I admired him long before we met. I appreciate everything he's done.

Leonard Goldberg: We had a film company together for a time, but imagine what would have happened if we started together when we were kids. We would have made billions!

Rich Cohen: Without him, no book. We had lots of fun,

and will have lots more. Thank you.

Tommy Armour, who has been like a son to me. I love him. Some of my best times in life are on the golf course with him.

Jonathan Karp, Cary Goldstein, and the team at Twelve: For helping me share my journey with the world.

Jessica Goodman, Dan Fellman, and the rest of the team at Warner Bros., and of course Kim Pinkstaff, who help me get it done.

Diana Jenkins: When I met Diana she was in her thirties, very young and beautiful, and still, I felt as if I was meeting Auntie Mame. She is wonderful. I hope I know her forever.

Lisa G.: You know who you are, and you know how much I love you.

Of course I want to thank my brother, Melvyn; his wife, Linda; and their family: Abby, Matt, Sofia, Richard, Meredith, and Jack. My children: Michael and his wife, Maria; Julie; Jamie and her husband, Jacoby; and Jody. My grandchildren, all of whom have names that come right out of the Bible, just like they do: Sarah, Rachel, Joseph, and Ari. My nieces, Keira and Kyla, and their parents, Mitchell and Donna. I love you all, and I am proud of you. Every generation bigger and stronger than the last, that's what I say.

Actors I Have Worked With

Casey Affleck
Karen Allen
Dan Aykroyd
Kevin Bacon
Ellen Barkin
Kim Basinger
Ned Beatty

Ralph Bellamy
Joey Bishop
Karen Black
Ronee Blakley
Jim Broadbent
George Burns
James Caan

Scott Caan
Sid Caesar
Mickey Callan
Keith Carradine
Vincent Cassell
Jackie Chan
Kyle Chandler
Geraldine Chaplin
Chevy Chase
Don Cheadle
Michael Chiklis
Julie Christie
George Clooney
Robbie Coltrane
Sean Connery
Tom Courtenay
Tom Cruise
Timothy Daly
Matt Damon
Beverly D'Angelo
Tony Danza
John Denver
Michael Douglas
Charles Durning
Shelley Duvall
Bob Einstein
Ethan Embry
Peter Falk
Ralph Fiennes
Albert Finney
Josh Flitter
Andy Garcia
Teri Garr
Henry Gibson

Isabel Glasser
Scott Glenn
Jeff Goldblum
Elliott Gould
Steve Guttenberg
Gene Hackman
Thomas Hulce
Eddie Izzard
Eddie Jemison
Martin Kove
Shelley Long
Jon Lovitz
Bernie Mac
Ralph Macchio
Lee Majors
Noriyuki "Pat" Morita
Michael Murphy
Craig T. Nelson
Wayne Newton
Marisol Nichols
Al Pacino
Brad Pitt
Donald Pleasence
Shaobo Qin
Randy Quaid
Carl Reiner
Paul Reiser
Molly Ringwald
Emma Roberts
Eric Roberts
Julia Roberts
Mickey Rourke
Jaden Smith
Elisabeth Shue

Henry Silva

Paul Sorvino

Sylvester Stallone

Rod Steiger

Daniel Stern

Sharon Stone

George Strait

Barbra Streisand

Hilary Swank

Richard Thomas

Uma Thurman

Lily Tomlin

Susan Tyrell

Lesley Ann Warren

Bruce Willis

Oprah Winfrey

James Woods

Joanne Woodward

Catherine Zeta-Jones

Clients and People I Promoted in the Management and Music Years

Paul Anka

Charles Aznavour

Shelley Berman

Joey Bishop

Pat Boone

Jackson Browne

Jimmy Buffett

George Burns

Harry Chapin

Eric Clapton

Joe Cocker

Alice Cooper

Charlie Daniels

Tony Danza

John Davidson

Mac Davis

John Denver

Neil Diamond

Bob Dylan

Dan Fogelberg

Peter Frampton

Connie Francis

Kinky Friedman

Jerry Garcia

Bobby Goldsboro

Dorothy Hamill

Uriah Heep

Florence Henderson

Don Imus

Waylon Jennings

Elton John

Shari Lewis & Lambchop

Gordon Lightfoot

Ed McMahon

Jimmy McNichols

Lee Majors

Barry Manilow

Bob Marley

Ian Matthews

Curtis Mayfield

Roger Miller

Joni Mitchell

Jane Morgan

Muppets

Michael Murphy

Wayne Newton

Ted Nugent

Robert Palmer

Tom Paxton

Robert Plant

Elvis Presley

Richard Pryor

Phil Ramone

Kenny Rogers

Mort Sahl

Boz Scaggs

Bob Seger

Frank Sinatra

Phoebe Snow

Rod Stewart

Steven Stills

Mary Travers

Frankie Valli

Sylvie Vartan

Joe Walsh

Barry White

Paul Williams

Edgar Winter

Chuck Woolery

Neil Young

Frank Zappa

Movies I Produced

1975 *Nashville*

1977 *September 30, 1955*

1977 *Oh, God!*

1980 *Cruising*

1981 *All Night Long*

1982 *Diner*

1984 *The Karate Kid*

1986 *The Karate Kid, Part II*

1987 *Happy New Year*

1988 *My Stepmother Is an Alien*

1989 *The Karate Kid, Part III*

1992 *Pure Country*

1994 *The Specialist*

1994 *The Next Karate Kid*

1997 *Vegas Vacation*

1998 *The Avengers*

1998 *Soldier*

2001 *Ocean's Eleven*

2004 *Ocean's Twelve*

2007 *Ocean's Thirteen*

2007 *Nancy Drew*

2010 *The Karate Kid*

Movies I Acted In

1993 *The Firm*, as Sonny Capps
1997 *Vegas Vacation*, as Jilly
2001 *Ocean's Eleven*, as High
     Roller
2002 *Confessions of a*
     Dangerous Mind, as Larry
     Goldberg

2004 *Full Frontal*, as Jerry
2004 *Ocean's Twelve*, as
     American Businessman
2007 *Ocean's Thirteen*, as
     Denny Shields

Directors and Writers I've Worked With

Robert Altman
Paul W.S. Anderson
Paul Attanasio
John G. Avildsen
Richard Benjamin
James Bridges
Christopher Cain
Jeremiah S. Chechik
George Clooney
Avery Corman
Andrew Fleming
William Friedkin
Larry Gelbart
Ted Griffin
Robert Mark Kamen
Stephen Kessler
Brian Koppelman
Alex Kurtzman
Richard LaGravenese

David Levien
Barry Levinson
Luis Llosa
Doug McGrath
Don MacPherson
Aline Brosh McKenna
George Nolfi
Robert Orci
David Webb Peoples
Sydney Pollack
Billy Ray
Carl Reiner
Gary Ross
Michael Soccio
Steven Soderbergh
Stephen Sommers
Joan Tewkesbury
Harald Zwart

Curriculum Vitae, or Attempt at Some Such

Bands and Groups I Promoted

Aerosmith

The Allman Brothers

The Association

Atlanta Rhythm Section

Average White Band

Bachman-Turner Overdrive
  (BTO)

Bad Company

The Beach Boys

The Bee Gees

Blue Oyster Cult

The Carpenters

Chicago

The Commodores

The Doobie Brothers

The Eagles

Earth, Wind & Fire

Foreigner

The Four Seasons

Grand Funk Railroad

The Grateful Dead

Guess Who

Hall & Oates

Heart

The Hudson Brothers

The Isley Brothers

Jethro Tull

The Kinks

Kiss

Led Zeppelin

Little Feat

Lynard Skynard

Marshall Tucker Band

The Moody Blues

New Birth

Ohio Players

The Pointer Sisters

Queen

Quicksilver
Rare Earth
REO Speedwagon
Seals & Crofts
Sonny & Cher
Starland Vocal Band
Steely Dan

Steve Miller Band
Thin Lizzy
Three Dog Night
War
Wings
Wright & Palmer
ZZ Top

About the Authors

Jerry Weintraub has spent more than five decades in show business, in the process earning a reputation as one of the savviest negotiators, smartest producers, and shrewdest film investors of our time. He has been praised and honored for his philanthropic work and, as UNICEF's Man of the Year, was presented with the organization's Danny Kaye Humanitarian Award.

Rich Cohen, a contributing editor at *Vanity Fair* and *Rolling Stone*, is the author of five books, including the bestsellers *Tough Jews, The Avengers,* and *Israel Is Real.* He lives in Connecticut with his wife, dog, and many masculine children.

INDEX

ABOUT TWELVE

TWELVE

TWELVE was established in August 2005 with the objective of publishing no more than one book per month. We strive to publish the singular book, by authors who have a unique perspective and compelling authority. Works that explain our culture; that illuminate, inspire, provoke, and entertain. We seek to establish communities of conversation surrounding our books. Talented authors deserve attention not only from publishers, but from readers as well. To sell the book is only the beginning of our mission. To build avid audiences of readers who are enriched by these works—that is our ultimate purpose.

For more information about forthcoming TWELVE books, please go to www.twelvebooks.com.